THE Stories OF THIS HOUSE

The Stories of This HOUSE

A Journal of What Makes Our House a Home

Sharon Naylor Toris

A TarcherPerigee Book

an imprint of Penguin Random House LLC
penguinrandomhouse.com

Copyright © 2022 by Sharon Naylor Toris
Penguin Random House supports copyright. Copyright fuels creativity, encourages diverse voices, promotes free speech, and creates a vibrant culture. Thank you for buying an authorized edition of this book and for complying with copyright laws by not reproducing, scanning, or distributing any part of it in any form without permission. You are supporting writers and allowing Penguin Random House to continue to publish books for every reader.

TarcherPerigee with tp colophon is a registered trademark of Penguin Random House LLC.

Most TarcherPerigee books are available at special quantity discounts for bulk purchase for sales promotions, premiums, fund-raising, and educational needs. Special books or book excerpts also can be created to fit specific needs. For details, write: SpecialMarkets@penguinrandomhouse.com.

ISBN 9780593539255
LCCN 2022935110

Printed in the United States of America
1st Printing

Book design by Shannon Nicole Plunkett

For Joe, who makes our house
so much more than a home every day

Acknowledgments

Joanna Ng brought this book to life. Have you ever just taken an enormous chance, hit Send, and wound up with more than you ever hoped for? That's how Joanna and I met, and that's how she was able to see the purpose in this book, the heart in it, and the deep importance I held for the memory of my parents. Thank you, Joanna, for every kindness along the way and for every bit of your editor magic.

Meredith Bernstein, my literary agent for so many years, guided this book into reality as well. She's family of my heart. I absolutely adore you, Meredith!

Christy Wagner brought polishing star power to my manuscript with her copyedit. I am forever grateful for your wisdom and eagle eye, Christy.

So many thanks to Shannon Plunkett, our masterful designer, who brought such magic and style to this book's design! Every adorable detail (including the kitten!) is Shannon's fabulousness, and I couldn't possibly be happier. Thank you.

Thank you to Katie Macleod-English for handling the marketing of this book with such care and enthusiasm, even when I burst out of the gate with an appearance idea months before anyone planned to get to that. I appreciate you!

Rachel Duggan's motivation in marketing and publicizing this book is a treasured part of our team, and again I feel like the luckiest girl ever to get to work with these and other fabulous experts at TarcherPerigee.

My parents had a lot to do with each of these ladies joining us for every moment of *The Stories of This House*'s creation and magic out in the world. You're here with us always.

Rob and Kathy, thank you for loving that house so well, and for inviting my husband and me to take a tour of your jaw-droppingly gorgeous renovations.

Joe, thank you for encouraging me to hit Send, and for always knowing that word I'm trying to remember but can't place. You always do. I love you every moment.

And my baby, Jinkx. You made us a family. I love you and Daddy tons. You're the best part of this house.

Contents

Introduction

There's something so wonderful about a quiet house.

The peace. The silence. The stillness. A breeze that smells like gardenias.

You can breathe.

The house breathes.

But it doesn't stay silent for long. This beautiful house of yours has stories to tell, some in the faintest of echoes, stories from every milestone celebration, every pair of champagne glasses clinked for love, every kiss in a doorway, every perfectly baked batch of cookies, every worry, every tear.

Your house holds more details of your wonderful life than you even know. A tiny bloom of affection. An adoring gaze cast upon you while you're making pancakes. It knows the moment you fell in love, when your miracles happened, and when your blessings arrived. Your house knows. And maybe you know and remember, too. If you wrote them down, that is.

Well, I post everything on Facebook or Instagram, so I have it all there, you may think. You do have stories. Stories set at hotels and beaches, by waterfalls, and at pumpkin patches or while swimming with dolphins, camping by the lake, or dancing at other people's weddings. These are fabulous stories, all of them, and they're wonderful to capture in any format.

What we want to capture here are the stories of your house, from the breathtaking, momentous occasions to quieter, simpler, golden moments of your life that mean so much but don't make it to your social media highlight reel. How a special day felt. What inspired your choices. Someone who brought their joy into your home. What you cooked for holidays or the average Tuesday. And we want it all to be in your handwriting.

Handwriting is such a treasure, and it gets more valuable every day. Do you know how much your family loves your handwriting? It's you, what so much of your love looked like on little notes and in every card. When we lose a loved one, or just miss them very much from a distance, we hold our own fingers above the space where that person's pen swirled and angled the words, feeling closer to them somehow. It's familiar, a soul-quenching comfort.

Real handwriting is everything.

I can tell you this from the heart. Several years ago, I had the honor (and tears, and pain, and exhaustion) of cleaning out my mother's home after she passed away. There is not a spoon, coaster, candle, or macaroni necklace from forty years ago that didn't pass through my hands. I was on an emotional shipwreck dive for weeks. The cleaning, the clearing, the donation pile, the recipes taking a place of honor safely far away from the recycling pile . . . and a little flash of gold caught my eye: *My Diary*. It was the gold lettering on the black cover of my mom's diary, which she began when she had me. Of all the journals she had kept in her life, this is the only one I found during the weeks of clearing out her home. I could say that all of the stories about me being an angel baby, sleeping through the night almost immediately, captivated me and that was sweet enough. But what really stood out was Mom's excitement about her new butter-yellow kitchen, the paint color inspired by a mango my father had picked for her during their honeymoon.

I had never heard that story before. Paint color inspiration? I'd never thought to ask. But I had the story now. In her words, lilting. I could "hear" the inflection of her voice, a little bit of a question at the end. It was her voice. And her love of colors. And my parents' love story. I had all of that back again. Because she wrote it down. Before age took her clarity and some of the stories floated away. Before grief over my dad's passing siphoned away so much of her joy. But there! I had her back now. Because she wrote it down.

I'll always be grateful, for that story and all the others she journaled and the sweet little things she kept and tucked away. That was the moment the idea for this book leapt into my heart, butter-yellow and smelling of gardenias. I would make this journal for you someday.

The Stories of This House is your time capsule to capture the wonderful little sights, sounds, tastes . . . the stuff that matters but that you don't post on social media. And here you are, ready to record so much about your life right here in this house, so you'll have every detail to look back on, and so your kids will have a little more of you in these pages.

Look ahead at the chapters to come. Pick your favorite topics and moments. Skip around in order of the path you set for yourself. The joy here is in your freedom to journal about your life in this house and the people and pets who made it a home.

And a fun little extra: I'll show you how to research the history of your house from before you even got there. Perhaps a fascinating character from fifty, sixty, or seventy years ago once walked your hallways and enjoyed the view from your kitchen window. Maybe your home was built on the site of something lovely, like a garden or farm. Perhaps your family can join in to find out the fascinating facts of your house and the land it sits on.

Over time, your house's makeovers show who you were and how you and your dreams have evolved. You'll find space here to journal about your home remodels, paint color evolutions, and landscape adventures, from pergolas to outdoor fireplaces to new baby Japanese maple trees that will change and grow. (Looking at before and after photos of trees we planted is one of my delights.) As you refresh your home, journal about it. Not just the hammer-and-nail parts, but also how you feel about the makeovers. About your child being old enough (what?!) to pick out paint colors. About that bright purple.

So much magic will live in this book. Feel free to use fun, colorful pens and stickers— whatever inspires you—as you make everlasting art of the living, breathing details of your life. Include favorite song lyrics, quotes, recipes, and more—all the good stuff.

I'm excited for you to fill these pages, and I'm happy for the magic it will bring to anyone, including you, who someday finds, reads, and loves everything about the stories of your house. Let's go.

Chapter 1

Buying This House

Many relationships start with a good how-they-met story, and there's likely so much magic in yours. So many things had to go just right to place you in the perfect spot to "meet" and fall in love with your house. Here, share the story of how you first "met" your house and how that love story grew.

How long did it take for this house to steal your heart? Was it love at first sight? Or did you flirt with a few other houses before fate took you by the shoulders and turned you this way?

_____

_____

Some people fall in love during the _approach_ to their house, gliding along majestically tree-lined streets with stunning sunset views and fall foliage. Perhaps a spotted fawn watches you from a small grove of trees, or horses look on from their pasture. Neighbors wave like they've known you for years as they push their strollers and walk their dogs. What kind of heaven is this? What was that first approach, or the first few approaches, like? How did the neighborhood make you feel at home?

_____

_____

_____

Or maybe this little house just needed some love . . . some new paint . . . a new porch . . . new windows . . . a new roof and new fencing. It was the house equivalent of the Charlie Brown Christmas tree, sad and slumping, but you knew it had so much potential. The first impression might have been scary, but now you're so glad you took the leap.

Here is where you'll record the story of buying this house, from first glance to final bid, popping champagne and carrying the first box through the front door.

Who was the first to find your house's listing? Where did you see it listed? Attach the original listing here or in the back of this book. You'll want it later for wowing future loved ones with the asking price, selling price, and what the house included.

_____

_____

_____

What was it that you loved most about the listing?

_____

_____

Was there anything in the listing that turned out to be misleading? Or surprising? Like a listed fourth bedroom that actually turned out to be a pantry?

_____

_____

_____

_____

Who would play your Realtor in a movie about this house?

_____

Who went to the first visit of this house?

_____

_____

What was the first thing you saw outside this house? Inside?

_____

_____

What were your first impressions?

_____

_____

_____

_____

Who was the first to say, "This is _it_! We're _home_."

_____

If it took a few visits to convince you, what finally won you over? Being there during the golden hour of perfect lighting outside, making slants of gilded rays across the floor? Maybe it was quiet and peaceful in the early evening hours, so different from where you lived at the time?

_____

_____

_____

_____

_____

What did you say your first projects would be?

_____

_____

First room to paint? _____

First demo? _____

First room to totally redo? _____

Did you tackle these projects right away, or has it been *years*? Did you ever get to them, or did other projects jump ahead in line? What were your actual first several projects?

_____

_____

_____

_____

_____

What was the first offer you made on the house?

_____

_____

Was there a bidding war? What did you think/adjust/accept to stay in the bidding war?

_____

_____

_____

What was the final price?

_____

What were some of the things the prior owners agreed to fix or add as part of your purchase?

_____

_____

_____

_____

_____

What were some signs that you chose well? A rainbow arching overhead after a downpour? A flock of cardinals flitting around the yard?

_____

_____

_____

Chapter 2

What the Original House Was Like

When you started pulling off paneling, tearing out carpet, steaming off wallpaper and borders, and revealing what was underneath the house's "shell," what did you find? Gorgeous original hardwood aching for refinishing? Stunning carvings above the fireplace? A message in a bottle tucked behind the drywall? On many HGTV remodeling shows, the person swinging the sledgehammer often reveals a hidden-for-years box of old photos, handwritten letters, maps or original blueprints of the house, yellowed newspaper clippings, or a section of wood pencil-marked with children's growing heights.

A home reveals itself to you layer by layer, trusting you with its secrets, its story freed from decades of being kept hidden. And some of those secrets can be sweet, such as a cloudy-edged Polaroid of the young couple who painted this room decades ago, stowed in the drop ceiling or inside a corner of the crown molding. A little hello from the past and a chance to see their faces.

Of course, sometimes the discovery is less than delightful, as in the case of carpet glued to the subfloor. Or, less frustrating, questionable orange, pirate-themed wallpaper behind the warped wood paneling, to go with the orange shag carpet removed from the playroom/soon-to-be home office. (This one was my house.)

Use these pages to document your house's unearthed secrets. You might never know the full stories behind those found photos, such as where that Polaroid couple is now, or who picked out the orange, pirate-themed wallpaper, but it's fascinating to look into a kind of time portal to see your home long ago.

What were your most fascinating finds? Feel free to attach photos!

DATE	FIND	LOCATION

Attach photos here.

What was your go-to lunch while demoing, painting, and fixing up your house? (Include the restaurant and your favorite order if it was takeout.)

Which songs come to mind from your demo playlist?

Who did which tasks, such as painting, sanding, etc.?

What was the best thing you found?

What was the worst thing you found?

If you kept these found treasures, where did you store them? Are they in a lockbox? In the closet safe? In a photo album?

_____

_____

_____

_____

_____

Over the years, you may find many additional "gifts" from within your house, little treasures that show you the house's past from days long before you got there, and also—wonderfully—from within your own years of living here. It's the archaeology of your home's life story. Keep it all, if you can. Your loved ones will marvel at it someday, as will you with every discovery.

Notes: _____

_____

_____

_____

_____

_____

_____

_____

Chapter 3

The Stories of Fixing This Space

After demo day and the tearing out of carpets, it's time to refresh, remodel, repaint, and redesign the rooms and spaces of your home. This is where your creativity soars, as colors and textures, not to mention entirely new open spaces, come alive as your house takes on an entirely new feeling, shape, and personality. Each space you make over, each glow-up that you design, takes its place here so you and future loved ones can see the beauty and magic you made in your home. And yes, it's going to be a time machine someday, with the colors that are so on-trend now looking entirely different in thirty years. You may end up laughing at the old styles the way some people laugh at 1980s hairstyles, or past trends may come back into fashion. Here is where you capture what you've created, and the world you made for your family.

For each home décor or remodel project in your house, record all the details here, including paint color names and what inspired you to pick that shade. It's the story behind the selection that stands out here, how the gift of an apricot-colored rose (named after Marilyn Monroe) inspired your kitchen's makeover, how the texture of a thrifted book's cover in a cool blue color inspired the upholstery of a couch, a baby's preference for a particular lilac-colored pillow directing the palette for her "big girl room" later on. Capture the inspirations here.

Some will impress. Some will amuse. Some will cause you to tilt your head in recollection, remembering what it was like to paint that room. Every second of it a treasure.

Rooms and Spaces to Capture

The remaining pages of this chapter give you space to record your home décor and remodel projects in all their beauty and style. Consider some of the following rooms that you may choose to freshen up and make your own. And yes, outdoor "rooms" and spaces count, too!

Kitchen

Dining room

Living room

Den

Master bedroom

Bedroom

Nursery

Home office

Basement

Garage and workshop

Laundry room

Front yard

Backyard

Deck, firepit, and pool area

Notes: _____

_____

_____

_____

_____

_____

Our Remodeled Room

Room: _____

Date: _____

What the room needed: _____

_____

_____

What the room got: _____

_____

_____

Describe your inspiration: _____

_____

Who designed it: _____

Who worked on it? And what did they work on? _____

_____

_____

Color combination: _____

_____

Color brands/names: _____

_____

Furniture and built-ins: _____

_____

_____

Attach photos here.

Appliances: _____

_____

_____

Windows: _____

_____

_____

Lighting: _____

_____

_____

Décor items: _____

_____

_____

_____

Your "Someday" wish list for this space: _____

_____

_____

_____

Your favorite parts of this space: _____

_____

_____

_____

_____

Our Remodeled Room

Room: _____

Date: _____

What the room needed: _____

_____

_____

What the room got: _____

_____

_____

Describe your inspiration: _____

_____

Who designed it: _____

Who worked on it? And what did they work on? _____

_____

_____

Color combination: _____

_____

Color brands/names: _____

_____

Furniture and built-ins: _____

_____

_____

Attach photos here.

Appliances: _____

_____

_____

Windows: _____

_____

_____

Lighting: _____

_____

_____

Décor items: _____

_____

_____

_____

Your "Someday" wish list for this space: _____

_____

_____

_____

Your favorite parts of this space: _____

_____

_____

_____

_____

Our Remodeled Room

Room: _____

Date: _____

What the room needed: _____

_____

_____

What the room got: _____

_____

_____

Describe your inspiration: _____

_____

Who designed it: _____

Who worked on it? And what did they work on? _____

_____

_____

Color combination: _____

_____

Color brands/names: _____

_____

Furniture and built-ins: _____

_____

_____

Attach photos here.

Appliances: _____

_____

_____

Windows: _____

_____

_____

Lighting: _____

_____

_____

Décor items: _____

_____

_____

_____

Your "Someday" wish list for this space: _____

_____

_____

_____

Your favorite parts of this space: _____

_____

_____

_____

_____

Our Remodeled Room

Room: _____

Date: _____

What the room needed: _____

_____

_____

What the room got: _____

_____

_____

Describe your inspiration: _____

_____

Who designed it: _____

Who worked on it? And what did they work on? _____

_____

_____

Color combination: _____

_____

Color brands/names: _____

_____

Furniture and built-ins: _____

_____

_____

Attach photos here.

Appliances: _____

_____

_____

Windows: _____

_____

_____

Lighting: _____

_____

_____

Décor items: _____

_____

_____

_____

Your "Someday" wish list for this space: _____

_____

_____

_____

Your favorite parts of this space: _____

_____

_____

_____

_____

Our Remodeled Room

Room: _____

Date: _____

What the room needed: _____

_____

_____

What the room got: _____

_____

_____

Describe your inspiration: _____

_____

Who designed it: _____

Who worked on it? And what did they work on? _____

_____

_____

Color combination: _____

_____

Color brands/names: _____

_____

Furniture and built-ins: _____

_____

_____

Attach photos here.

Appliances: _____

_____

_____

Windows: _____

_____

_____

Lighting: _____

_____

_____

Décor items: _____

_____

_____

_____

Your "Someday" wish list for this space: _____

_____

_____

_____

Your favorite parts of this space: _____

_____

_____

_____

_____

Chapter 4

What We Planted Here

See that maple tree by the end of the driveway? The forty-footer? We planted that the weekend we moved into this house. It was barely two feet high. And the photos prove that the little scrawny tree that looked like a mistake grew into this gorgeous, majestic giant.

Here you'll note your landscaping talents (and luck) as you record any trees, bushes, bulbs, and arbors you put in. You might have to think back a few years to recall previous plantings.

Your First Plantings

What was the first thing you planted when this house became yours? Temporary things like vincas and fall mums count!

_____

_____

_____

_____

What was the first "This has got to go" plant you had removed from the prior owners' landscaping?

_____

What were the happy surprises you found already planted here when you moved in?

_____

_____

_____

_____

_____

What was the most disappointing planting you found, or something you thought you could save but couldn't?

_____

_____

_____

_____

_____

_____

Who planted those bulbs that come up every year?

_____

_____

_____

_____

Your Trees

Which kinds of trees did you plant at this house over the years?

_____

_____

_____

Are any trees "special," like an anniversary gift that you planted together for your fifth anniversary? Are any trees gifts from other people?

_____

_____

_____

Did you have a tree house? Or a tree swing?

_____

_____

Any there memorable stories about the trees in your yard, like the tree your kids used to climb? Or a limb that came down during a storm and your neighbor helped cut it and clear it away?

_____

_____

_____

_____

What hung in those trees? Birdhouses? Hummingbird feeders?

_____

_____

_____

_____

Who designed your gardens and landscape? And who did the heavy labor, like the shoveling, the lifting, and the planting?

_____

_____

_____

_____

Who were your gardening helpers? For instance, if your kids helped, what did they do?

_____

_____

_____

_____

_____

Attach any garden inspiration images here,
along with your before and after landscape photos.

Your Vegetable and Herb Garden

What's been planted in your garden? For many people, a lush garden checks an important box on their dream home wish list. Your garden may have thrived (a worthy story for your house!) or struggled (more worthy stories for your house!). A year with a bumper crop of limes set you up for margaritas . . . and then there were some lime trees that looked like they were about to deliver but the squirrels got all but one fruit.

Gardening is a passion, one that can be shared with the whole family, and here is where you'll record your veggie and herb garden victories—the crops that got taken over by a hornet's nest, or the chili peppers that were too hot for you but the neighbors would come over and take all they wanted . . . which is when you found out the neighbor's four-year-old son ate those super-fiery peppers that you can't handle. Yet you kept planting them every year because the kid loved them.

Here are your favorite, most thriving, garden selections:

Vegetables: _____

_____

_____

_____

_____

_____

Herbs: _____

_____

_____

_____

_____

Fruits: _____

_____

_____

_____

_____

_____

Greens: _____

_____

_____

_____

_____

_____

Fruit trees: _____

_____

_____

_____

_____

_____

Wanting to switch things up, you might plant a collection of herbs essential to a theme, such as a salsa garden with several different kinds of tomatoes, tomatillos, cilantro, jalapeño and serrano peppers, onions, and garlic. These basics turn out a bounty of so many different kinds of salsa for your family's cooking joy. What kinds of themed gardens did you have at your house?
(Pesto, Greek salad, hummus ingredient garden, pizza toppings garden, etc.)

Describe any garden features that meant a lot to you, such as a garden bench where you spent quiet time reading or meditating. Share images of personalized garden path stones, or of your dreamy little hammock nook with lilting tree fronds and a bubbling garden fountain.

Attach photos of your garden mishaps and/or victories here.

Chapter 5

Stories of the Neighborhood

Let's take a look at your neighborhood, which likely played some part in your happiness during these years, and if not, well . . . then you likely have some interesting stories about it.

If your neighborhood has plenty of charm and personality, neighbors who have become friends or even more like family, kids in Halloween costumes crunch-stepping on autumn leaves, and neighbor dogs you know by name, then there's some of the magic in your life.

Be sure to record neighbors by first and last names to help both your memory years from now and your future loved ones who may want to ask them about the neighborhood, the town, and any memories or FYIs they would share.

Who were the first neighbors you met when you moved in?

_____

_____

_____

_____

_____

Who were some of the special neighbors you socialized with, maybe helped with their home projects or watched their pets for the weekend?

_____

_____

_____

_____

_____

Describe your block's social events. Were there block parties, dinner parties, tailgate parties, or Super Bowl or other sports parties?

_____

_____

_____

_____

_____

Which neighbors saved the day, such as by showing up with their teens and snow shovels to help dig you out of a big snowstorm?

_____

_____

_____

_____

_____

What are some fascinating facts about your neighbors?

_____

_____

Who's lived here the longest? _____

_____

Who has the coolest job? Like working for a TV show or for the FBI, running the best home

sales parties, being an author, or playing music at a brewery on the weekends?

_____

_____

What do they always bring to parties? _____

_____

_____

Who always has the big holiday party, the one you can always count on being the best bash

of the year? _____

_____

_____

Who goes all out when decorating their home for holidays? _____

_____

_____

Who has the most enviable garden or landscaping? _____

_____

_____

Whose recipes do you ask for most often? _____

_____

_____

Which kids are the best friends to your kids? Any stories about impressions they made

on you? _____

_____

_____

_____

_____

_____

Who are the mischievous kids in the neighborhood? Any stories about their mischief?

_____

_____

_____

_____

_____

_____

Attach photos of the neighborhood through the years, as you are able.
Spaces change, new houses go up, old houses get additions,
and new views take shape.

What else is amazing about your neighbors? What makes you love them so much?

_____

_____

_____

_____

_____

What about the animals? Which kinds of wildlife would you regularly see in your yard?

Any one-time sightings of rare animals or birds? _____

_____

_____

_____

_____

_____

Notes: _____

_____

_____

_____

_____

_____

_____

Chapter 6

Events That Took Place Here

Sometimes home is the perfect place for special events. A big event adds to the soul of your house, as the celebration itself fills you with joy and the memories live on as if they have seeped into every surface, every inch of your home, and even the air around it. Special events breathe even more life into your home.

Here, you'll record some of the most amazing events that happened at home, who was with you, what was on the menu, what the décor looked like, and as many details about the celebration as you'd like to remember.

Share standout memories from the following celebrations.

Your Housewarming Party

Date: _____

Who was here: _____

_____

_____

_____

_____

Party style (alfresco dinner, barbecue, brunch, etc.): _____

Décor highlights: _____

_____

Menu (appetizers, mains, and sides): _____

_____

_____

_____

_____

_____

Drinks: _____

_____

Desserts: _____

_____

Special additions: _____

_____

Anniversary Party

Date: _____

Who was here: _____

_____

_____

_____

_____

Party style (alfresco dinner, barbecue, brunch, etc.): _____

Décor highlights: _____

_____

Menu (appetizers, mains, and sides): _____

_____

_____

_____

_____

_____

Drinks: _____

_____

Desserts: _____

_____

Special additions: _____

_____

Someone Is Popping the Question! Here!

Date: _____

Who was here: _____

_____

_____

_____

_____

Party style (alfresco dinner, barbecue, brunch, etc.): _____

Décor highlights: _____

_____

Menu (appetizers, mains, and sides): _____

_____

_____

_____

_____

_____

_____

Drinks: _____

_____

Desserts: _____

_____

Special additions: _____

_____

Bridal or Couple's Shower

Who it was hosted for: _____

Date: _____

Who was here: _____

_____

_____

_____

_____

Party style (alfresco dinner, barbecue, brunch, etc.): _____

Décor highlights: _____

_____

Menu (appetizers, mains, and sides): _____

_____

_____

_____

_____

Drinks: _____

_____

Desserts: _____

_____

Special additions: _____

_____

Rehearsal Dinner

Date: _____

Who was here: _____

_____

_____

_____

_____

Party style (alfresco dinner, barbecue, brunch, etc.): _____

Décor highlights: _____

_____

Menu (appetizers, mains, and sides): _____

_____

_____

_____

_____

_____

Drinks: _____

_____

Desserts: _____

_____

Special additions: _____

_____

At-Home Wedding

Who it was hosted for: _____

Date: _____

Who was here: _____

_____

_____

_____

_____

Party style (alfresco dinner, barbecue, brunch, etc.): _____

Décor highlights: _____

_____

Menu (appetizers, mains, and sides): _____

_____

_____

_____

_____

Drinks: _____

_____

Desserts: _____

_____

Special additions: _____

_____

Wedding Weekend Party

Date: _____

Who was here: _____

_____

_____

_____

_____

Party style (alfresco dinner, barbecue, brunch, etc.): _____

Décor highlights: _____

_____

Menu (appetizers, mains, and sides): _____

_____

_____

_____

_____

_____

Drinks: _____

_____

Desserts: _____

_____

Special additions: _____

_____

Deployment Gathering

Date: _____

Who was here: _____

_____

_____

_____

_____

Party style (alfresco dinner, barbecue, brunch, etc.): _____

Décor highlights: _____

_____

Menu (appetizers, mains, and sides): _____

_____

_____

_____

_____

Drinks: _____

_____

Desserts: _____

_____

Special additions: _____

_____

Homecoming (School, Deployment, Lengthy World Travels, Work Assignments, etc.)

Date: _____

Who was here: _____

_____

_____

_____

_____

_____

Party style (alfresco dinner, barbecue, brunch, etc.): _____

Décor highlights: _____

_____

Menu (appetizers, mains, and sides): _____

_____

_____

_____

_____

Drinks: _____

_____

Desserts: _____

_____

Special additions: _____

_____

Baby Shower

Date: _____

Who was here: _____

_____

_____

_____

_____

Party style (alfresco dinner, barbecue, brunch, etc.): _____

Décor highlights: _____

_____

Menu (appetizers, mains, and sides): _____

_____

_____

_____

_____

_____

Drinks: _____

_____

Desserts: _____

_____

Special additions: _____

_____

Baby's First Visitors

Date: _____

Who was here: _____

_____

_____

_____

_____

Party style (alfresco dinner, barbecue, brunch, etc.): _____

Décor highlights: _____

_____

Menu (appetizers, mains, and sides): _____

_____

_____

_____

_____

_____

Drinks: _____

_____

Desserts: _____

_____

Special additions: _____

For more baby events and firsts, go to Chapter 8, "Kids' Moments."

High School Graduation

Date: _____

Who was here: _____

_____

_____

_____

_____

Party style (alfresco dinner, barbecue, brunch, etc.): _____

Décor highlights: _____

_____

Menu (appetizers, mains, and sides): _____

_____

_____

_____

_____

_____

Drinks: _____

_____

Desserts: _____

_____

Special additions: _____

_____

Kids Departing for College

Date: _____

Who was here: _____

_____

_____

_____

_____

Party style (alfresco dinner, barbecue, brunch, etc.): _____

Décor highlights: _____

_____

Menu (appetizers, mains, and sides): _____

_____

_____

_____

_____

_____

Drinks: _____

_____

Desserts: _____

_____

Special additions: _____

_____

Celebrating Big Accomplishments

Congratulations! Perhaps you got a promotion, launched your own business, or earned an advanced degree or a professional certification. When you've added some extra letters after your name, chalked up some additional titles, launched your dream-come-true business, or achieved a momentous goal, it's time to celebrate! And your house may be your chosen home for the party.

Use these pages to capture everything you loved about the special occasion, and especially how they came about, because big accomplishment festivities are often *surprises* planned by loved ones. Perhaps you've planned some of these for your loved ones. Surprise or not, the memory of these festive occasions lives in your house for a long time. You all felt so much love and support here.

There is such goodness in this house.

Promotion

Date: _____

Who was here: _____

_____

_____

_____

Party style (alfresco dinner, barbecue, brunch, etc.): _____

Décor highlights: _____

Menu (appetizers, mains, and sides): _____

_____

_____

Drinks: _____

Desserts: _____

Special additions: _____

Earning an Advanced Degree or Certification

Date: _____

Who was here: _____

_____

_____

_____

_____

Party style (alfresco dinner, barbecue, brunch, etc.): _____

Décor highlights: _____

_____

Menu (appetizers, mains, and sides): _____

_____

_____

_____

_____

_____

Drinks: _____

_____

Desserts: _____

_____

Special additions: _____

_____

Starting a Business

Date: _____

Who was here: _____

_____

_____

_____

_____

_____

Party style (alfresco dinner, barbecue, brunch, etc.): _____

Décor highlights: _____

_____

Menu (appetizers, mains, and sides): _____

_____

_____

_____

_____

_____

Drinks: _____

_____

Desserts: _____

_____

Special additions: _____

_____

Big Firsts for Each of You

A big first might be more in the sentimental lane. It might be smaller in scope than the culmination of years devoted to earning a master's degree or launching a business, but it's still meaningful to you. For instance, maybe you've finally gotten your dream car, the one you've saved for for years. Maybe you've always wanted to see your favorite singer in concert and it finally happened. Maybe you made the perfect soufflé for the first time, or learned how to make sushi at home.

Every fabulous first counts! And what a window each is into the person you are now (and someday, it'll be a window into the person you were *then*), so these are some of the most treasured memories in this book.

In the chart below, record the fabulous firsts for each member of the family accomplished while living at this house. And let your loved ones know that they can write in any of their own firsts here. Feel free to slide more pages of firsts into this journal if you run out of space. Someday, finding them might add to the joy of discovery within these pages.

FAMILY MEMBER	BIG FIRST	DATE	WHY IT MEANS SO MUCH

FAMILY MEMBER	BIG FIRST	DATE	WHY IT MEANS SO MUCH

Special Moments with Special People

I love this section.

Spending time with parents, grandparents, and other treasured elders on the branches of your family tree is always a special event. Sitting with them, talking, cooking, or taking in the pretty sky at sunset from a patio couch with a pitcher of warm cider on the side table can be the best thing ever. Time with older generations is a gift, and this book helps you capture those wonderful moments.

Use this space to write about your together time, your most memorable chats, and what these special people were like.

TOGETHER TIME WITH: _____

Attach photos and notes.

TOGETHER TIME WITH: _____

Attach photos and notes.

TOGETHER TIME WITH: _____

Attach photos and notes.

And siblings? They count, too, and you may find that they've grown even more precious to you over the years.

In twenty years, you'll be glad you journaled about the fun times at home with your siblings, like making midnight snacks from Thanksgiving leftovers while you were a little bit tipsy, or dressing up to go out on New Year's Eve. Or even just sitting outside together, not doing anything.

TOGETHER TIME WITH: _____

Attach photos and notes.

TOGETHER TIME WITH: _____

Attach photos and notes.

TOGETHER TIME WITH: _____

Attach photos and notes.

Add notable stories of people you first met at your house, such as at a party. Perhaps a couple met here at your tailgate party, hit it off, and their own stories are now unfolding . . .

Attach photos and handwritten notes, emails, or texts about the wonderful things that took place in your home.

Chapter 7

What We Were Like in This House

If someone asked you, *"What were you like in this house?"* what would your answer be?

We were adored, and we knew it. We experienced unconditional love.

We had so much fun, always!

We always had some tensions, and our strong-willed family members often butted heads. But we loved one another. Maybe we didn't like one another every minute, but if any of us needed anything, it only took one phone call.

Perhaps it's a mix of these, with—of course—some space for everyone's realities.

So let's start with the big question, and you can fill in as many answers as it takes to get the gist of what you all felt.

What were you like in this house? _____

Now let's scale down from the big picture to a more granular view: What were you like when you were having fun together? When you took part in family traditions?

This section aims to capture family events, rituals, game nights, and other moments that brought you together, adding to the stories of your house. Family recipes. TV shows you all couldn't wait to watch together every week. Cultural practices. A cherished lullaby your grandmother used to sing to you that you then sang to your kids in this house. These are all the little things that are so much more than little things in your life. It's precisely these details that mean the world to you and that you want to share with future loved ones who pick up this book, hoping to learn more about you and the life you all lived here. They make up the answer to, *"What was it really like to live here?"*

So let's look at those family traditions and weekly group "dates," perhaps to remember a time when everyone was together, happy, playing, and participating . . . and perhaps to restart those family traditions.

Family Traditions

SUNDAY DINNER

Sunday-night dinners may have been full of your family's favorite dishes or cultural dream menus like pasta and meatballs, braciola, garlic bread, salad with a homemade vinaigrette. Or perhaps Sunday dinners included Southern masterpieces like chicken and ribs, potato salad, cornbread and hush puppies, collards, and sweet potato pie. Whatever says "Sunday dinner" to you, load up this page like a heaping bowl of pasta with all of the details that went into your Sunday dinner traditions.

Menu (appetizers, mains, and sides): _____

_____

Drinks: _____

Desserts: _____

Sunday dinner table settings and décor: _____

Playlist: _____

Extra details: _____

Attach photos here.

WEEKEND BRUNCH

Stack up the waffles and fry the bacon crispy the way you like it, as family brunch throws open the doors to the kitchen or takes the party outside. Weekend brunch can be the fuel for your family's activity-filled day—eat the pancakes; nosh some fruit; sip a green smoothie; and head out to the stadium, park, or trails for the day's events. Or it can be your post-event reward— let's say your family woke up early, ran a charity 5K, and now everyone's showered and changed for the postrace brunch. Brunch either fuels you or replenishes spent fuel, and that's why cooking together and sharing the meal is so special. Life may take you in different directions, but you all come back together for good food and good company.

Menu (appetizers, mains, and sides): _____

_____

Drinks: _____

Desserts: _____

Brunch table settings and décor: _____

Playlist: _____

Extra details: _____

Attach photos here.

COOKING PREP PARTIES

Some family events call for cooking and baking big batches of treats. Perhaps you need to make several dozen cupcakes or intricately ice six dozen cookies for a school event. Maybe you're making casseroles and meal baskets for a family friend who is ill or has suffered a loss. The family comes together in the kitchen, turns up the music, and assembles the recipes, watching the timer, extracting perfectly cooked dishes from the oven, and putting creative flair into packaging the culinary creations.

Sometimes the dream and design of a remodeled kitchen takes into account just these kinds of all-hands-on-deck family cooking hours. Food prep is a way to show love, and one of your family rituals may be cooking together for others.

Think back to some of the most memorable group food prep parties held in your kitchen.

What was the occasion? _____

Who was there? _____

_____

Who brought the recipes and supplies? _____

_____

Additional details: _____

Attach photos here.

FAMILY GAME NIGHT

Family game night brings together your crew for some good-natured competition, lots of laughs, a spread of snacks, and the chance to declare champions, as runners-up plot their strategies (and revenge!) for next time. Game night is also a chance to get everyone to unplug, step away from screens, and reconnect with family and friends.

Do you have that one favorite game that is synonymous with game night? Maybe it's "Monopoly night" or "Clue night" in your family? Do the little ones join in for "Hungry Hungry Hippos night"? Or do you fire up the game system and virtually travel together to your favorite dystopian nightmare to battle aliens as a family? Whatever you play, switching it up each time or sticking with what works, game night may have grown into a big deal with themed snacks and drinks . . . or just some brownies.

What games are your favorites? _____

_____

Who in the family wins most frequently? _____

Who gets the sportsmanship award? _____

How did your game night change, if it did, as the kids grew up? _____

_____

_____

If you let game night slide for a season, perhaps when kids went off to school or during a health crisis or family support time, how did you reinstate game night for all? _____

_____

_____

_____

What are your signature snacks and drinks? _____

_____

_____

For championship games, such as the final round of a tournament you planned, what are the prizes? _____

_____

Any other game night memories to share here? _____

_____

_____

_____

_____

Attach photos here.

POOL PARTIES

Turn up the steel drum music, blend some frozen daiquiris or piña coladas, fire up the grill for juicy burgers and just-barely-split hot dogs, and coat yourself with sunscreen, and no matter where you are, you'll feel an island breeze of sorts. Instead of BYOB, this pool party is BYOF (bring your own floaties) with everyone's funny, themed inflatable floats filling the swimming pool for unstructured fun in the sun.

Menu (appetizers, mains, and sides): _____

_____

_____

Drinks: _____

Desserts: _____

Décor: _____

Playlist: _____

Games: _____

_____

Extra details: _____

_____

Attach photos here.

How did your pool area change over the years? Did you replace your above-ground pool with a stunning in-ground pool? Add a hot tub? Install an outdoor kitchen and party zone with an alfresco fireplace, pizza oven, and sound system? Capture the before and after photos here.

Attach photos here.

SUPER BOWL, PLAYOFF GAMES, AND OTHER SPORTS PARTIES

When it's time for the big games, the family tradition of pregame parties and watching the excitement on the big-screen TV can be taken to a whole new level. No one would dare miss a Super Bowl party featuring your standout menu, a full bar, and Super Bowl–themed cakes.

Some families keep a tradition of making the same signature, high-demand menu items such as buffalo wings, mini meatballs, jalapeño poppers, layered dips, and Dad's signature ribs. Plus mini pizzas for the kids. And some, of course, just order a stack of pizzas. Some might roll in a keg, and some might pour specialty drinks in team colors. Big-game party hosts tend to pull out all the stops for football fetes, and their parties become legendary.

If, as it was with my parents, the Super Bowl was *everything* as the center of our entertaining universe, filling out this section can perhaps inspire you to call back the family from wherever they're scattered now to have a "Throwback Super Bowl Bash" with everyone's favorites on the buffet table.

I can just hear my dad now: "You made enough food for an army!" Makes me smile every time. He was the happiest guy in the buffet line. Steamed lobster, crab, Swedish meatballs, Korean beef sticks, sloppy joe sandwiches, a monster tray of Italian pastries . . . and that was just the pregame spread. Round two would be on the way soon after. Those were the best times.

GAME/EVENT: _____

Menu (appetizers, mains, and sides): _____

_____

_____

Drinks: _____

Desserts: _____

Décor: _____

Playlist: _____

Games: _____

_____

Extra details: _____

_____

Attach photos here.

GAME/EVENT: _____

Menu (appetizers, mains, and sides): _____

_____

_____

Drinks: _____

Desserts: _____

Décor: _____

Playlist: _____

Games: _____

_____

Extra details: _____

_____

Attach photos here.

GAME/EVENT: _____

Menu (appetizers, mains, and sides): _____

_____

_____

Drinks: _____

Desserts: _____

Décor: _____

Playlist: _____

Games: _____

_____

Extra details: _____

_____

Attach photos here.

The Holidays

What is your favorite holiday? It is, of course, perfectly fine to declare them all winners and consider yourselves the lucky family that can get together to celebrate in so many ways.

Many dishes on the holiday table check boxes of happiness and comfort. Your grandmother's sage stuffing. Your mom's chocolate mousse. Your husband's cranberry sauce.

In these pages, record everything you've loved about holidays in this house, from the traditions you've brought into your home that were passed down through the generations to those you've created for yourselves.

> This book includes prompts about the holiday dishes that are loved by all generations, those that won't be invited back onto your menu next year, and those I-can-laugh-about-it-now dish fails. It's these unexpected outcomes that make for some of the best stories of your house. So don't count out those mistakes or flawed recipes, an unwise replacement ingredient, or a delivery that didn't arrive in time. Those plans that went awry can be some of the best stuff in your stories.

THANKSGIVING

Thanksgiving brunch or dinner—just the thought of it makes you want to put on stretchy-waist pants and look forward to the nap and the leftovers afterward as much as the meal itself. This is one of those holidays that stretches out its gifts, giving you days of traditions, from putting together your menu; to assigning dishes for relatives to bring; to shopping for, prepping, cooking, and styling a table full of dishes worthy of a lifestyle magazine photoshoot.

The wine flows, the turkey elicits satisfied *mmmm*s, and so many loved ones are embraced in a heartwarming scene of love and nurturing.

How does your family pile on the traditions? Who makes which delectable dishes and dreamy desserts? Start here with each person's signature dishes.

NAME	THEIR SPECIALTY THANKSGIVING MENU ITEM(S)

Does everyone own the most cherished family recipes? Where would they find them? In a parent's online folder? Is it password protected? Record the username and password here. It may be completely new information to loved ones flipping through this book that your parents even have a recipe folder.

_____

_____

_____

_____

_____

_____

_____

_____

_____

_____

_____

_____

If you have stored your menus online, attach each year's Thanksgiving menu in the following pages. How fun to get the story of how the menu never changed over the years, or to see how your menu shifted when family members became vegan or discovered a gluten intolerance. Even if it's on a printout or scan, any additional handwritten notes you add will create a deeper sense of personal connection.

Fill in your Thanksgiving musts, moments, and memories.

Thanksgiving

Year: _____

Who was here: _____

_____

_____

Menu (appetizers, mains, and sides): _____

_____

_____

Drinks: _____

Desserts: _____

Dishes everyone loved: _____

Dishes not invited back next year: _____

Kitchen scene: _____

Dish rescues: _____

Dish fails: _____

Décor: _____

Playlist: _____

What was your favorite pre-meal moment? _____

_____

What was your favorite post-meal moment? _____

_____

What else stands out? _____

Thanksgiving

Year: _____

Who was here: _____

_____

_____

Menu (appetizers, mains, and sides): _____

_____

_____

Drinks: _____

Desserts: _____

Dishes everyone loved: _____

Dishes not invited back next year: _____

Kitchen scene: _____

Dish rescues: _____

Dish fails: _____

Décor: _____

Playlist: _____

What was your favorite pre-meal moment? _____

_____

What was your favorite post-meal moment? _____

_____

What else stands out? _____

Thanksgiving

Year: _____

Who was here: _____

_____

_____

Menu (appetizers, mains, and sides): _____

_____

_____

Drinks: _____

Desserts: _____

Dishes everyone loved: _____

Dishes not invited back next year: _____

Kitchen scene: _____

Dish rescues: _____

Dish fails: _____

Décor: _____

Playlist: _____

What was your favorite pre-meal moment? _____

_____

What was your favorite post-meal moment? _____

_____

What else stands out? _____

Thanksgiving

Year: _____

Who was here: _____

_____

_____

Menu (appetizers, mains, and sides): _____

_____

_____

Drinks: _____

Desserts: _____

Dishes everyone loved: _____

Dishes not invited back next year: _____

Kitchen scene: _____

Dish rescues: _____

Dish fails: _____

Décor: _____

Playlist: _____

What was your favorite pre-meal moment? _____

_____

What was your favorite post-meal moment? _____

_____

What else stands out? _____

What else happens on Thanksgiving? Is there a high school football game in the morning, where the whole family goes either to play or to cheer on the participants while sipping on hot chocolate? Is it your family tradition to watch the Macy's Thanksgiving Day Parade, taking in previews of the top Broadway shows? Is mealtime followed by washing dishes, naps, and football watching, rounded out by grazing on leftovers and watching a movie together?

People dream about this kind of family Thanksgiving. Capture that magic. Write it all down.

Attach photos here.

CHRISTMAS, HANUKKAH, KWANZA, AND OTHER WINTER HOLIDAYS

The winter holidays may be marked by shopping sprees and lots of events taking place outside of your house, but the holiday spirit starts at home and fills the hearts of those here with joy, gratitude, good thoughts, and good deeds.

Again, as with Thanksgiving, you may prefer to plan the same menu each year. Everyone depends on your mom's lobster bisque, and don't you dare ever change it. Certain dishes bring us back to the foundations of our family lineage, and even if we make that bisque a little bit healthier than its yesteryear version with a brick of butter and multiple cups of heavy cream, it still counts as our beloved anchor to where our hearts are hung.

Use these pages to record the many ways that the winter holidays helped form your life in this house and tether your family members to one another.

Notes: _____

_____

_____

_____

_____

_____

_____

_____

_____

_____

_____

_____

_____

Winter Holiday Celebrations

Year: _____

Who was here: _____

_____

_____

Menu (appetizers, mains, and sides): _____

_____

_____

Drinks: _____

Desserts: _____

Dishes everyone loved: _____

Dishes not invited back next year: _____

Kitchen scene: _____

Dish rescues: _____

Dish fails: _____

Décor: _____

Playlist: _____

What was your favorite pre-meal moment? _____

_____

What was your favorite post-meal moment? _____

_____

What else stands out? _____

Winter Holiday Celebrations

Year: _____

Who was here: _____

_____

_____

Menu (appetizers, mains, and sides): _____

_____

_____

Drinks: _____

Desserts: _____

Dishes everyone loved: _____

Dishes not invited back next year: _____

Kitchen scene: _____

Dish rescues: _____

Dish fails: _____

Décor: _____

Playlist: _____

What was your favorite pre-meal moment? _____

_____

What was your favorite post-meal moment? _____

_____

What else stands out? _____

Winter Holiday Celebrations

Year: _____

Who was here: _____

_____

_____

Menu (appetizers, mains, and sides): _____

_____

_____

Drinks: _____

Desserts: _____

Dishes everyone loved: _____

Dishes not invited back next year: _____

Kitchen scene: _____

Dish rescues: _____

Dish fails: _____

Décor: _____

Playlist: _____

What was your favorite pre-meal moment? _____

_____

What was your favorite post-meal moment? _____

_____

What else stands out? _____

Winter Holiday Celebrations

Year: _____

Who was here: _____

_____

_____

Menu (appetizers, mains, and sides): _____

_____

_____

Drinks: _____

Desserts: _____

Dishes everyone loved: _____

Dishes not invited back next year: _____

Kitchen scene: _____

Dish rescues: _____

Dish fails: _____

Décor: _____

Playlist: _____

What was your favorite pre-meal moment? _____

_____

What was your favorite post-meal moment? _____

_____

What else stands out? _____

WHO MADE THAT SIGNATURE HOLIDAY DISH?

For the holidays, my grandmother made an apple strudel that was heaven. None of us can figure out which of the many apple strudel recipes in my departed grandmother's recipe collection is *the* holiday strudel. She may have doctored it with some extra flavor in the icing. No one knows. So prevent that kind of lost recipe disaster by recording here who makes that dish everyone loves, so when anyone wants the recipe, you've got a direct line to the chef.

NAME	SIGNATURE DISH

What are *your* signature dishes, drinks, and desserts? Imagine how happy your loved ones might be someday when they chance upon this collection of your famous, cherished recipes! Consider each to be a treasure, passed along with love and great memories.

Attach photos or recipes here.

What else is special about your family's holiday celebrations in this house?

_____

_____

Any night-before rituals?

_____

_____

Any morning-of rituals?

_____

_____

What are the symbolic décor items you look forward to displaying each year?

_____

_____

Describe your holiday prep party, when close friends and family arrive early to cook, decorate, and help out. Or perhaps a preholiday gift-wrapping or holiday craft-making party. Do you have a special menu of snacks and signature cocktails for these days?

_____

_____

_____

Do you do a secret Santa or white elephant gift exchange?

_____

Are you the hosts of the neighborhood holiday sweater party everyone wants an invite to?

_____

_____

What else about the holidays gives your family those "most wonderful time of the year" vibes?

_____

_____

What was the best winter holiday celebration you ever had in this house?

_____

_____

Any funny stories of holiday mishaps? Perhaps a missed flight or forgotten gift? A winter holiday proposal or pregnancy announcement?

_____

_____

_____

Anything else about the holidays you'd like to add to these stories of your house?

_____

_____

_____

If you have an extra-special holiday card that means the world to you, like the last card you received from your adored great-aunt before she passed away, or one with handwritten magic from your grandmother, grandfather, or a departed loved one, keep it safe. Place it in a frame to join your holiday décor, or secure it in this book.

Attach cards here.

NEW YEAR'S EVE

What's your New Year's Eve tradition? Hosting a soiree at your house? Staying in your pajamas, bingeing a Netflix series, and falling asleep before midnight?

_____

_____

How did you ring _out_ the old year?

_____

_____

How did you make your wishes and plans for the new year?

_____

_____

Any memorable New Year's celebrations in this house?

_____

_____

What was the best New Year's you've ever had in this house?

_____

_____

Any we-can-laugh-about-it-now New Year's experiences in this house?

_____

_____

New Year's Eve Celebrations

Year: _____

Who was here: _____

_____

_____

Menu (appetizers, mains, and sides): _____

_____

_____

Drinks: _____

Desserts: _____

Dishes everyone loved: _____

Dishes not invited back next year: _____

Kitchen scene: _____

Dish rescues: _____

Dish fails: _____

Décor: _____

Playlist: _____

What was your favorite pre-meal moment? _____

_____

What was your favorite post-meal moment? _____

_____

What else stands out? _____

New Year's Eve Celebrations

Year: _____

Who was here: _____

_____

_____

Menu (appetizers, mains, and sides): _____

_____

_____

Drinks: _____

Desserts: _____

Dishes everyone loved: _____

Dishes not invited back next year: _____

Kitchen scene: _____

Dish rescues: _____

Dish fails: _____

Décor: _____

Playlist: _____

What was your favorite pre-meal moment? _____

_____

What was your favorite post-meal moment? _____

_____

What else stands out? _____

New Year's Eve Celebrations

Year: _____

Who was here: _____

_____

_____

Menu (appetizers, mains, and sides): _____

_____

_____

Drinks: _____

Desserts: _____

Dishes everyone loved: _____

Dishes not invited back next year: _____

Kitchen scene: _____

Dish rescues: _____

Dish fails: _____

Décor: _____

Playlist: _____

What was your favorite pre-meal moment? _____

_____

What was your favorite post-meal moment? _____

_____

What else stands out? _____

New Year's Eve Celebrations

Year: _____

Who was here: _____

_____

_____

Menu (appetizers, mains, and sides): _____

_____

_____

Drinks: _____

Desserts: _____

Dishes everyone loved: _____

Dishes not invited back next year: _____

Kitchen scene: _____

Dish rescues: _____

Dish fails: _____

Décor: _____

Playlist: _____

What was your favorite pre-meal moment? _____

_____

What was your favorite post-meal moment? _____

_____

What else stands out? _____

VALENTINE'S DAY

Red heart candy boxes, champagne, a weekend away, diamonds . . . Record memories of the Valentine's Days you've lived in this house that really brought the romance, love, and appreciation.

_____

_____

_____

What were your favorite stay-at-home Valentine's Day celebrations, like a midnight picnic by the fireplace or a surprise meal cooked for you by your sweetheart or the kids?

_____

_____

Share about your favorite Valentine's Day family traditions.

_____

_____

What was your favorite Valentine's Day breakfast? Breakfast in bed, perhaps?

_____

_____

What was your favorite Valentine's Day grand gesture, like a special gift, a surprise, or the announcement of going on a big trip maybe?

_____

_____

_____

Valentine's Day Parties

Year: _____

Who was here: _____

_____

_____

Menu (appetizers, mains, and sides): _____

_____

_____

Drinks: _____

Desserts: _____

Dishes everyone loved: _____

Dishes not invited back next year: _____

Kitchen scene: _____

Dish rescues: _____

Dish fails: _____

Décor: _____

Playlist: _____

What was your favorite pre-meal moment? _____

_____

What was your favorite post-meal moment? _____

_____

What else stands out? _____

Valentine's Day Parties

Year: _____

Who was here: _____

_____

_____

Menu (appetizers, mains, and sides): _____

_____

_____

Drinks: _____

Desserts: _____

Dishes everyone loved: _____

Dishes not invited back next year: _____

Kitchen scene: _____

Dish rescues: _____

Dish fails: _____

Décor: _____

Playlist: _____

What was your favorite pre-meal moment? _____

_____

What was your favorite post-meal moment? _____

_____

What else stands out? _____

Don't forget about your kids' Valentine's Day memories. How did you make Valentine's Day a celebration for them?

If your kids gave out little Valentine's Day cards to the other children in their class, attach one here to get those great handwritten signatures of your youngsters in this book.

What was your all-time-favorite Valentine's Day memory in this house?

ST. PATRICK'S DAY

If your family is among those who gather in town centers and on city streets, awaiting the St. Patrick's Day Parade, with plans to gather after the parade for a party at your place, your home becomes imbued with Irish pride.

The party's at your place every year. Everyone loves your Irish stew, and your corned beef sandwiches and potatoes are second to none. The beer flows, and the cupcakes with green icing have just a smidge of Guinness in them.

Here, you can record the best parts of this holiday that took place at your house. Those who look back on this chapter will hear you bursting with joy about how great it smells in your kitchen as the corned beef cooks, how lovely the claddagh flutes look on the mantel, and how much your little ones love the holiday as well. St. Patrick's Day is a through line for your family, one of the many threads of identity that they've all grown to love through you. And even if you're not Irish and this is not your ancestral holiday, you will still be admired for how much you put into honoring *other people's* culture.

Here, share what this holiday is like for you and yours.

Notes: _____

_____

_____

_____

_____

St. Patrick's Day Parties

Year: _____

Who was here: _____

_____

_____

Menu (appetizers, mains, and sides): _____

_____

Drinks: _____

Desserts: _____

Dishes everyone loved: _____

Dishes not invited back next year: _____

Kitchen scene: _____

Dish rescues: _____

Dish fails: _____

Décor: _____

Playlist: _____

Games: _____

What was your favorite pre-meal moment? _____

_____

What was your favorite post-meal moment? _____

_____

What else stands out? _____

St. Patrick's Day Parties

Year: _____

Who was here: _____

_____

_____

Menu (appetizers, mains, and sides): _____

_____

Drinks: _____

Desserts: _____

Dishes everyone loved: _____

Dishes not invited back next year: _____

Kitchen scene: _____

Dish rescues: _____

Dish fails: _____

Décor: _____

Playlist: _____

Games: _____

What was your favorite pre-meal moment? _____

_____

What was your favorite post-meal moment? _____

_____

What else stands out? _____

EASTER, PASSOVER, AND OTHER SPRING HOLIDAYS

The earth is refreshing itself with flowers, lawns of fresh green grass, trees full of new leaves, and beautiful skies, and the spring holidays brighten your house with colorful décor, springtime outfits for the little ones, and family gatherings. If Easter is part of your celebration, do you plan an Easter egg hunt on the lawn for the family and neighborhood kids? Do you host the spring holidays with wonderful meals, wine, and sweet desserts? Record it all here to capture your spring festivities.

Attach photos here.

Spring Holiday Celebrations

Year: _____

Who was here: _____

_____

_____

Menu (appetizers, mains, and sides): _____

_____

Drinks: _____

Desserts: _____

Dishes everyone loved: _____

Dishes not invited back next year: _____

Kitchen scene: _____

Dish rescues: _____

Dish fails: _____

Décor: _____

Playlist: _____

Games: _____

What was your favorite pre-meal moment? _____

_____

What was your favorite post-meal moment? _____

_____

What else stands out? _____

Spring Holiday Celebrations

Year: _____

Who was here: _____

_____

_____

Menu (appetizers, mains, and sides): _____

_____

Drinks: _____

Desserts: _____

Dishes everyone loved: _____

Dishes not invited back next year: _____

Kitchen scene: _____

Dish rescues: _____

Dish fails: _____

Décor: _____

Playlist: _____

Games: _____

What was your favorite pre-meal moment? _____

_____

What was your favorite post-meal moment? _____

_____

What else stands out? _____

Spring Holiday Celebrations

Year: _____

Who was here: _____

_____

_____

Menu (appetizers, mains, and sides): _____

_____

Drinks: _____

Desserts: _____

Dishes everyone loved: _____

Dishes not invited back next year: _____

Kitchen scene: _____

Dish rescues: _____

Dish fails: _____

Décor: _____

Playlist: _____

Games: _____

What was your favorite pre-meal moment? _____

_____

What was your favorite post-meal moment? _____

_____

What else stands out? _____

Spring Holiday Celebrations

Year: _____

Who was here: _____

_____

_____

Menu (appetizers, mains, and sides): _____

_____

Drinks: _____

Desserts: _____

Dishes everyone loved: _____

Dishes not invited back next year: _____

Kitchen scene: _____

Dish rescues: _____

Dish fails: _____

Décor: _____

Playlist: _____

Games: _____

What was your favorite pre-meal moment? _____

_____

What was your favorite post-meal moment? _____

_____

What else stands out? _____

MOTHER'S DAY AND FATHER'S DAY CELEBRATIONS IN THIS HOUSE

How did you celebrate the moms and dads, stepmoms and stepdads, and all other parental figures in your lives? As time goes by, families grow and change, and when celebratory dates pop up on the calendar, festivities may have filled your home with love, gratitude, and favorite memories.

Mother's Day

Year: _____

Who was here: _____

_____

Menu (appetizers, mains, and sides): _____

_____

_____

Drinks: _____

Desserts: _____

Dishes everyone loved: _____

Dishes not invited back next year: _____

Kitchen scene: _____

Dish rescues: _____

Dish fails: _____

Décor: _____

Playlist: _____

What was your favorite pre-meal moment? _____

What was your favorite post-meal moment? _____

What else stands out? _____

Mother's Day

Year: _____

Who was here: _____

_____

_____

Menu (appetizers, mains, and sides): _____

_____

_____

Drinks: _____

Desserts: _____

Dishes everyone loved: _____

Dishes not invited back next year: _____

Kitchen scene: _____

Dish rescues: _____

Dish fails: _____

Décor: _____

Playlist: _____

What was your favorite pre-meal moment? _____

_____

What was your favorite post-meal moment? _____

_____

What else stands out? _____

Father's Day

Year: _____

Who was here: _____

_____

_____

Menu (appetizers, mains, and sides): _____

_____

_____

Drinks: _____

Desserts: _____

Dishes everyone loved: _____

Dishes not invited back next year: _____

Kitchen scene: _____

Dish rescues: _____

Dish fails: _____

Décor: _____

Playlist: _____

What was your favorite pre-meal moment? _____

_____

What was your favorite post-meal moment? _____

_____

What else stands out? _____

Father's Day

Year: _____

Who was here: _____

_____

_____

Menu (appetizers, mains, and sides): _____

_____

_____

Drinks: _____

Desserts: _____

Dishes everyone loved: _____

Dishes not invited back next year: _____

Kitchen scene: _____

Dish rescues: _____

Dish fails: _____

Décor: _____

Playlist: _____

What was your favorite pre-meal moment? _____

_____

What was your favorite post-meal moment? _____

_____

What else stands out? _____

SUMMER HOLIDAYS: MEMORIAL DAY, 4TH OF JULY, AND LABOR DAY

If you have a summer beach house; if your family visits a resort, quaint bed and breakfast, or lake house each year; or if you go on an annual family camping trip or cruise, *wherever you are is home to you on that trip so it counts for this book*. The summer vacation memories you make, like any vacation, contribute to the life you're living in this house, your home base.

How often do you vacation during the summer? Every weekend? One or two big trips? Or is the backyard pool it for you?

Summer holidays open your home and yard for parties, especially if your house is "the gathering house" and your cooking and barbecuing are on everyone's request list. Did you go to the town parade each Memorial Day or 4th of July? What did you love about that? The town picnic with the three-legged races and petting zoo? The beer garden? The antique cars chauffeuring veterans from the Greatest Generation down the main thoroughfare? Your at-home celebration might follow this town tradition as you and your favorite neighbors celebrate together at your place.

Notes:

_____

_____

_____

_____

_____

_____

_____

_____

_____

_____

_____

Summer Parties

Year: _____

Who was here: _____

_____

_____

Menu (appetizers, mains, and sides): _____

_____

Drinks: _____

Desserts: _____

Dishes everyone loved: _____

Dishes not invited back next year: _____

Kitchen scene: _____

Dish rescues: _____

Dish fails: _____

Décor: _____

Playlist: _____

Games: _____

What was your favorite pre-meal moment? _____

_____

What was your favorite post-meal moment? _____

_____

What else stands out? _____

Summer Parties

Year: _____

Who was here: _____

_____

_____

Menu (appetizers, mains, and sides): _____

_____

Drinks: _____

Desserts: _____

Dishes everyone loved: _____

Dishes not invited back next year: _____

Kitchen scene: _____

Dish rescues: _____

Dish fails: _____

Décor: _____

Playlist: _____

Games: _____

What was your favorite pre-meal moment? _____

_____

What was your favorite post-meal moment? _____

_____

What else stands out? _____

Summer Parties

Year: _____

Who was here: _____

_____

_____

Menu (appetizers, mains, and sides): _____

_____

Drinks: _____

Desserts: _____

Dishes everyone loved: _____

Dishes not invited back next year: _____

Kitchen scene: _____

Dish rescues: _____

Dish fails: _____

Décor: _____

Playlist: _____

Games: _____

What was your favorite pre-meal moment? _____

_____

What was your favorite post-meal moment? _____

_____

What else stands out? _____

Summer Parties

Year: _____

Who was here: _____

_____

_____

Menu (appetizers, mains, and sides): _____

_____

Drinks: _____

Desserts: _____

Dishes everyone loved: _____

Dishes not invited back next year: _____

Kitchen scene: _____

Dish rescues: _____

Dish fails: _____

Décor: _____

Playlist: _____

Games: _____

What was your favorite pre-meal moment? _____

_____

What was your favorite post-meal moment? _____

_____

What else stands out? _____

Summer Parties

Year: _____

Who was here: _____

_____

_____

Menu (appetizers, mains, and sides): _____

_____

Drinks: _____

Desserts: _____

Dishes everyone loved: _____

Dishes not invited back next year: _____

Kitchen scene: _____

Dish rescues: _____

Dish fails: _____

Décor: _____

Playlist: _____

Games: _____

What was your favorite pre-meal moment? _____

_____

What was your favorite post-meal moment? _____

_____

What else stands out? _____

HALLOWEEN

Were you the house with dozens of spooky mannequins and special effects lighting on your lawn? Oversized spiders crawling up your house? Various hands eerily emerging from the ground? Those who love to decorate and style scary scenes for trick-or-treaters or for their Halloween party love the fall holiday season. Pay tribute to the Halloweens that happened at your house here.

Attach photos here.

Who took on the lead role as Halloween décor designer and engineer?

_____

What did you *make* to add to your house's Halloween décor?

_____

_____

_____

Which Halloween décor items are you the proudest of?

_____

_____

Did you ever win a prize in a neighborhood Halloween décor contest?

_____

_____

What were your Halloween treats like? Full-sized candy bars? Minis? Stickers and toys?

_____

_____

What were some of the best Halloween costumes your family wore?

_____

_____

_____

_____

Attach photos here.

Did your pets wear Halloween costumes?

_____

_____

Attach photos here.

Did you host Halloween parties? For adults or for kids? Share the details of your Halloween parties here.

_____

_____

_____

_____

_____

_____

_____

_____

Halloween Parties

Year: _____

Who was here: _____

_____

_____

Menu (appetizers, mains, and sides): _____

_____

Drinks: _____

Desserts: _____

Dishes everyone loved: _____

Dishes not invited back next year: _____

Kitchen scene: _____

Dish rescues: _____

Dish fails: _____

Décor: _____

Playlist: _____

Games: _____

What was your favorite pre-meal moment? _____

_____

What was your favorite post-meal moment? _____

_____

What else stands out? _____

Halloween Parties

Year: _____

Who was here: _____

_____

_____

Menu (appetizers, mains, and sides): _____

_____

Drinks: _____

Desserts: _____

Dishes everyone loved: _____

Dishes not invited back next year: _____

Kitchen scene: _____

Dish rescues: _____

Dish fails: _____

Décor: _____

Playlist: _____

Games: _____

What was your favorite pre-meal moment? _____

_____

What was your favorite post-meal moment? _____

_____

What else stands out? _____

Halloween Parties

Year: _____

Who was here: _____

_____

_____

Menu (appetizers, mains, and sides): _____

_____

Drinks: _____

Desserts: _____

Dishes everyone loved: _____

Dishes not invited back next year: _____

Kitchen scene: _____

Dish rescues: _____

Dish fails: _____

Décor: _____

Playlist: _____

Games: _____

What was your favorite pre-meal moment? _____

_____

What was your favorite post-meal moment? _____

_____

What else stands out? _____

Halloween Parties

Year: _____

Who was here: _____

_____

_____

Menu (appetizers, mains, and sides): _____

_____

Drinks: _____

Desserts: _____

Dishes everyone loved: _____

Dishes not invited back next year: _____

Kitchen scene: _____

Dish rescues: _____

Dish fails: _____

Décor: _____

Playlist: _____

Games: _____

What was your favorite pre-meal moment? _____

_____

What was your favorite post-meal moment? _____

_____

What else stands out? _____

Additional Holidays and Observances

Daughter's Day. Son's Day. Pet's Day. Instagram and Facebook remind you of holidays all the time, giving you good reason to celebrate. So if you connect to Daughter's Day or any other chosen holiday, here is where you can share how you celebrated those days.

> For any holiday or observance, it's the meaning to your family that matters most. You have your cherished ways of planning your traditions and rituals, and if you decide to try something new, even what doesn't take off for your family and friends can become a great story.

CULTURAL CELEBRATIONS

Whatever your heritage, you very likely have cultural traditions that you and your family celebrate, in small ways and in big, splashy, party-hosting ways. It can be as simple as adding pierogies to your holiday menu, giving your carb base a nod to your heritage. Your kids get to absorb some of your cultural pride, and your parents beam, knowing that you've embraced their family rituals.

Think curries from India.

Tapas, paella, and jamón from Spain.

Tacos al pastor from Mexico.

Sushi and tempura from Japan.

Any cultural celebration in your house will incorporate the famous dishes of that region; your group might stick to the expected dishes or plan an adventurous dinner that features some new-to-you cuisine made authentically at eateries around town. Food trucks may be your chosen portal to international foods. You might not want to try your hand at making them, but instead trust the pros to make those foods safely and authentically. It's a nice way to try new foods and support local businesses as well.

Cultural celebrations also include dance. Tangos. Native American dances to hypnotic drumbeats, the dancers mesmerizing as they move in rhythm together. Perhaps your family has been known to watch videos of different types of dancing and have a dance lesson night.

Record all the details of your cultural explorations here.

Celebration

Year: _____

Who was here: _____

_____

_____

Menu (appetizers, mains, and sides): _____

_____

_____

Drinks: _____

Desserts: _____

Décor: _____

Playlist: _____

Games: _____

Prizes: _____

Other notes and favorite things: _____

_____

_____

_____

_____

_____

_____

Your family may investigate your culture online and find out that you share a heritage you might not have expected. To explore this aspect of your identity, check out the cuisine of your ancestors, dance as if in their shoes, and attempt their cultural traditions like hygge. If you explored your heritage's vistas and tastes, record what you have found here.

_____

_____

_____

_____

_____

_____

_____

_____

_____

_____

_____

_____

_____

_____

_____

_____

_____

CELEBRATORY MEALS

Speaking of food, what are some of your family's favorite celebratory meals? Perhaps you like to lay out some lengths of kraft paper on the backyard deck table and dump out on it a bushel of steamed lobsters and crabs, plus corn on the cob and baked potatoes, for a family clambake. Think back on special meals like this, and for future iterations, note what you'd add to the menu, how you'd set the party up differently, which drink pairings you'd make, and sweet treats to close the party right.

Attach photos here.

Celebratory Meal

Year: _____

Who was here: _____

_____

_____

_____

Menu (appetizers, mains, and sides): _____

_____

_____

_____

_____

Drinks: _____

Desserts: _____

Décor: _____

Playlist: _____

Toasts and tributes: _____

_____

Gifts: _____

_____

Your favorite aspect of this celebratory meal: _____

_____

_____

Celebratory Meal

Year: _____

Who was here: _____

_____

_____

_____

Menu (appetizers, mains, and sides): _____

_____

_____

_____

_____

Drinks: _____

Desserts: _____

Décor: _____

Playlist: _____

Toasts and tributes: _____

_____

Gifts: _____

_____

Your favorite aspect of this celebratory meal: _____

_____

_____

Celebratory Meal

Year: _____

Who was here: _____

_____

_____

_____

Menu (appetizers, mains, and sides): _____

_____

_____

_____

_____

Drinks: _____

Desserts: _____

Décor: _____

Playlist: _____

Toasts and tributes: _____

_____

Gifts: _____

_____

Your favorite aspect of this celebratory meal: _____

_____

_____

Celebratory Meal

Year: _____

Who was here: _____

_____

_____

_____

Menu (appetizers, mains, and sides): _____

_____

_____

_____

_____

Drinks: _____

Desserts: _____

Décor: _____

Playlist: _____

Toasts and tributes: _____

_____

Gifts: _____

_____

Your favorite aspect of this celebratory meal: _____

_____

_____

EVERYDAY MEALS

Some of the most important moments of your life in this house will be experienced around the kitchen table, with no party going on, no holiday meals being prepped. Just you all, a meatloaf, and some peas. It may seem challenging to record anything of value from this scenario, but once you start, it's like your view of the night sky slowly comes into focus: where once you saw nothing, so many tiny dots of stars and planets begin coming into focus.

Let's look at everyday meals.

Who's at the table?

_____

_____

Where are you seated, and why do your meals take place there?

_____

_____

_____

Is the TV on, is music playing, are family members on their phones . . . or have you established that family mealtime is quiet connection time?

_____

_____

What's the best thing about family meals at the table?

_____

_____

_____

Ask the family which are their favorite . . .

Comfort meals: _____

_____

_____

Delivery meals: _____

_____

_____

Fancy meals: _____

_____

_____

Healthy meals: _____

_____

_____

Barbecue meals: _____

_____

_____

Other meals and food choices: _____

_____

Recipes You Love Most

During all the years of living in this house, some very special recipes have delighted your tastes and created nurturing meals for your family. Perhaps traditional recipes take you back in time to when you shared the table with relatives who are no longer with you. Perhaps a certain recipe won someone's heart, and they're now a regular in your home and at your table. A recipe may have sprung from a challenging time, such as when a parent or a child faced a health challenge or a particularly bad flu, and this chicken soup "doctored" with some turmeric and barley set them on the road to recovery.

Your recipes have stories, too.

Throughout this book, you likely thought about family favorite recipes as you reflected on different holidays and celebrations and the meals served on those special days. In the Halloween section, your mind may have traveled to that amazing "severed finger" hot dog casserole everyone Instagrammed before diving in. Thinking about tailgate parties may have had your mouth watering for your signature red pepper hummus. Recipes just fit in everywhere; they're sensory markers in your memories.

Recipes come to you as gifts from relatives. You may find yourself the recipient of a treasured family recipe that your uncle never gave out, not to anyone . . . until you got married and moved into this house, when your uncle decided that his wedding gift to you would be his secret recipe.

In ancestors' found journals, you may discover the purest of treasures: handwritten recipes on softened, yellowed paper, stained with sauces and oils from when they were used long ago. Recipes are family gold. You'll pass them down, or your kids will look for them in your house someday, holding your recipes up to the light with tears in their eyes for all of the heartfelt memories they hold.

I found my mother's recipes as well as her tattered journal when I was cleaning out her house after her death, and the notes she wrote in the margins of typed recipes told such fabulous stories: *"No! Use ¼ the sugar!" "Don't forget to put some oil on your hands so that the ground lamb doesn't stick."* And this one brought the tears: Mom wrote "Just for me" on a chocolate cookie recipe. Entire novels have been written about mysterious notes on recipes, and I sat there cross-legged on the dining room floor, looking at that recipe written on the back of a scrap of wrapping paper. Red-and-white candy cane–striped wrapping paper with a cookie recipe messily scribbled in pen and smudged, as if she were rushing to get the directions just right before leaving a holiday party.

For some reason, Mom thought no one else would love that cookie recipe, or maybe she was so overwhelmed during the holidays and with the pressures of being a young mom and hard-working homemaker that she just wanted a little something for *her*. She wasn't the type to roll her eyes and say, "For a change." She just had a remarkable sense of discernment and knew she deserved some self-kindness decades before self-care became a Thing.

That's a lot of wonderful story in a curled-up little scrap of wrapping paper with smudged writing on it.

Attach your favorite recipes from this home here, and record why those recipes and the memories they evoke mean so much to you.

Recipe: _____

Who is this recipe from? _____

What is the story of this recipe? _____

_____

Include the recipe below: _____

_____

_____

_____

_____

_____

_____

_____

_____

_____

Recipe: _____

Who is this recipe from? _____

What is the story of this recipe? _____

_____

_____

Include the recipe below: _____

_____

_____

_____

_____

_____

_____

_____

_____

_____

_____

_____

_____

_____

_____

Recipe: _____

Who is this recipe from? _____

What is the story of this recipe? _____

_____

_____

Include the recipe below: _____

_____

_____

_____

_____

_____

_____

_____

_____

_____

_____

_____

_____

_____

_____

_____

Recipe: _____

Who is this recipe from? _____

What is the story of this recipe? _____

_____

_____

Include the recipe below: _____

_____

_____

_____

_____

_____

_____

_____

_____

_____

_____

_____

_____

_____

_____

Recipe: _____

Who is this recipe from? _____

What is the story of this recipe? _____

_____

_____

Include the recipe below: _____

_____

_____

_____

_____

_____

_____

_____

_____

_____

_____

_____

_____

_____

Recipe: _____

Who is this recipe from? _____

What is the story of this recipe? _____

_____

_____

Include the recipe below: _____

_____

_____

_____

_____

_____

_____

_____

_____

_____

_____

_____

_____

_____

_____

Recipe: _____

Who is this recipe from? _____

What is the story of this recipe? _____

_____

_____

Include the recipe below: _____

_____

_____

_____

_____

_____

_____

_____

_____

_____

_____

_____

_____

_____

_____

_____

Recipe: _____

Who is this recipe from? _____

What is the story of this recipe? _____

_____

_____

Include the recipe below: _____

_____

_____

_____

_____

_____

_____

_____

_____

_____

_____

_____

_____

_____

_____

_____

Recipe: _____

Who is this recipe from? _____

What is the story of this recipe? _____

_____

_____

Include the recipe below: _____

_____

_____

_____

_____

_____

_____

_____

_____

_____

_____

_____

_____

_____

_____

_____

_____

Recipe: _____

Who is this recipe from? _____

What is the story of this recipe? _____

_____

_____

Include the recipe below: _____

_____

_____

_____

_____

_____

_____

_____

_____

_____

_____

_____

_____

_____

Activities and Interests

As with the "Everyday Meals" section, sometimes it's the routine moments that build closeness, a sense of belonging, and comfort at home. There's more going on than just making some popcorn, dimming the lights, getting in front of the TV, and watching a movie together. It's a shared experience that can be especially meaningful when you have a tradition of watching a series and you all are invested in the characters. You are totally immersed in their world. Just like being at home.

Here is where you can record some of your family's favorite shared entertainment. When your family watches your show, it's a touchpoint in your week. It gives you something to look forward to and something to talk about afterward.

Years from now, you're going to enjoy being reminded of these shows, movies, books, concerts, and more that color your time spent in this house. And yes, concerts count, even though they don't occur in your home or backyard. When you gather together before and after the event, such as fixing some snacks or leftovers at 2 a.m. after the concert, it's an event in this house. You can always make your own rules about what to include in this journal.

What are your favorite TV shows to watch together in this house?

_____

_____

_____

_____

_____

What are your kids' favorite shows to watch in this house?

_____

_____

_____

_____

What are your favorite new movies that you watched for the first time in this house?

_____

_____

_____

What are your favorite old movies to watch for perhaps the twentieth time together?

_____

_____

_____

Who are your favorite celebrities you'd watch in anything you could find?

_____

_____

_____

What about seasonal programming? Are there holiday movies you always have to watch together? Do you watch *every* holiday movie on the Hallmark Channel, wearing your Hallmark Christmas Movie–themed socks and T-shirts, sipping from your signature wineglass or hot chocolate mug, and munching on gourmet popcorn?

_____

_____

_____

_____

GAMING

Gaming systems are not just for kids; adults have their own gaming systems that offer a little treat and reward in their hectic lives. The kids might not even be aware that when Mom is working in her home office, she actually might be building a virtual island oasis, or fighting off bad guys, or donning a superhero's costume to take out some supervillains.

Perhaps you game together with your family members, as adversaries or as one group fighting for the same justice. However gaming exists in your world, don't count it out as a source of important stories in this house. Gaming may provide an essential means of connecting with your preteen during those challenging years of growth. Together, you relax and befriend each other. No one is judging or missing opportunities to be present with one another.

Here, share what gaming has brought to you and your family, and add those excellent details of which games you all love the most.

What are some favorite games you play together?

_____

_____

Does your gaming fanhood extend to gaming conferences? Have you attended or dressed up? (Photos, please!)

_____

Attach photos here.

SPORTS

Sports mean excitement, adrenaline, and passion for fans, and when the game is on, everyone in your family gathers together in their jerseys, team logo cupcakes on the table, chili bubbling on the stove. It doesn't have to be the Super Bowl for you to feature an impressive spread of food and snacks. All eyes are glued to the plays and replays that make the game great. Is there anything better than an impossible catch made blind over the shoulder? Your group jumps to their feet, high fives one another, marvels "How did he *do* that?!" The defender was holding, but there's no flag. Your group launches into shouts at the ref, decrying the outrage. Emotions just *fly* when you're all watching the game. Isn't it *great*?

Think about the impact that watching sports has had on your life here in this house. From football to soccer, golf to tennis, and every sport in between, your family and friends all love their favorite teams and athletes. Why else would someone walk into the room and ask, "How are *we* doing?" to check on the score. We belong to our team. We belong to the great circle of fans and superfans. As a family, we may all love the same team, or we may each have our own favorites, bringing a fun, competitive atmosphere to the house. ("*You're going down!*")

If you're a sports-fan family, you have a fabulous shared passion filling this house, with so many memories from games, miracle wins, and near-comebacks.

Before you begin journaling, be sure you're looking at all angles of sports-fan life, from college sports that bring you big-time rivalries to high school sports that bring your family to the local high school field as you cheer on your own child or a relative, your school spirit on full display. You're all great fans.

Record your sports fan life here.

Where you watch:

_____

How many screens do you have on if you watch multiple games at the same time?

_____

Who are your family members' favorite teams and players?

_____

Do you all dress up in team jerseys and T-shirts? Do the kids dress up, too?

What's on the menu (appetizers, meal, sides)?

What's on the bar list?

What's for dessert?

Do you decorate for every game, or just for playoff and championship games?

Who is your sports expert, the person everyone asks about penalties, plays, and players?

What's the best thing about watching games with your family in this house?

Don't forget . . . *you* may be the athletes.

You might run a marathon, compete in a swim meet, or play softball or baseball. With your family there to lend their support and cheer you on, you're elated as you cross the finish line or beat your personal best time. In the stands, your family and friends go nuts. In addition to trophies and medals, you bring that excitement back home with you.

This is a house where winners live, where great effort is expended, where you overcome and come back, where you shine. In this house you receive comfort after bad games and mistakes. In this house the people you love tell you—and show you—they believe in you.

Record all you feel about being a sports fan and a sports family in this house.

_____

_____

Which sports do you play or practice here at your house?

_____

_____

I love this question! I was the *worst* at softball. During games, I'd pick flowers out in right field, and I couldn't hit a ball to save my life. But when it was just me and my dad in the backyard practicing after dinner, with him pitching to me, my bat connected *hard* every time. The ball sailed into the woods behind our house again and again. I just loved being out there with my dad and no pressure. I could journal about those moments endlessly.

Your family might go out back to play touch football or volleyball. You all just like one another's company, and you find so many ways to play together, to spend time together. *This is the good stuff in your journal.* Record how your family's least-gifted player is treated like a star when he or she triumphs, when that ball sails into the woods even once.

Share how your house is home to games, good-natured or competitive.

_____

_____

_____

BOOKS

We read all of the Harry Potter books together.

Rainy days were for snuggling and reading children's books we got from the library.

My son just discovered a love of reading! My book club friends have recommended some series he might be interested in.

That half hour before bed is my reading time, when I dive headfirst into romance novels and historical fiction.

Books fill our hearts, and the words sink into our souls. As readers, we travel through time, meet fascinating people, and learn about different time periods and customs. Some of your favorite memories in this house will revolve around reading books, so record here the books you most love and share in this house.

What are your favorite memories of reading together as a family? Reading a book series? Just quiet time together, with everyone reading their own choices?

_____

_____

_____

_____

_____

What are some favorites books recommended to you by others?

_____

_____

_____

_____

_____

What are some books that you read *and* then enjoyed as a TV series, miniseries, or movie?

_____

_____

_____

What are your book club memories in this house?

_____

_____

_____

What are your kids' favorite memories related to books in this house?

_____

_____

_____

Did you have a favorite reading nook or cozy chair by the fireplace, perfect for getting lost in a novel?

_____

What are some books that you'd love to read again as a family, here in this house?

_____

_____

_____

_____

ARTS, CRAFTS, AND MAKER PASSIONS

What did you make in this house? Did you build a garden trellis from reclaimed wood? Did you brew your own beer? Were you into mosaic art? Did you paint portraits or sculpt? Affix bits of sea glass in a frame to make it look like a brown dog and a bright-blue butterfly? Did you make floral wreaths for your doors?

This house has been home to artists. Creators. Makers. What did you bring to life here? What did your kids discover artistically? Were they into writing and drawing comic books, a childhood art interest that eventually led to a career in comics publishing, that all started on a little desk in the kitchen, next to the kitchen island, with crayons and glue sticks?

Perhaps you and your daughter made crystal bracelets and necklaces to sell at the church's holiday bazaar or in her Etsy shop.

Record here what each of you loved to create . . . and you know what? Forget about quantifying your sales and reviews. Just write about what it was like to create in this house, to be inspired here, to love what you were making. Just the joy of being an artist.

What was it like to create art in this house?

_____

_____

_____

_____

What were some of the things you made on your own?

_____

_____

_____

_____

_____

What were some of the things you made with your family members in this house?

_____

_____

_____

_____

_____

What were some art projects that amusingly didn't go your way? They may have been frustrating at the time, but now it's a great story!

_____

_____

_____

_____

_____

Do you have any art projects that you keep even now as a treasured possession? Anything handed down to you, or made by an artist loved one?

_____

_____

_____

_____

_____

Our Favorite People in This House

Your house has been filled with the love of your family, the people who live within its walls. But isn't your house so immeasurably lucky to welcome your closest friends, your kids' friends, and their families, too? And don't forget the much-appreciated helpers like babysitters, nannies, and dog-walkers, who bring *their* light, assistance, and comfort to your house. Add in the people who help your house run smoothly, like housecleaning specialists, repair technicians, and the mail carrier. These folks are doing their jobs, yes, but they also choose to be kind to you. If they see that you're on crutches, for example, they're going to bring your trash cans in from the curb.

Journal about who has come to your house, bringing with them the kind of special treatment that makes them feel like friends or even family.

Who are some of your favorite people who spend time here?

_____

_____

_____

Who would you be happy to have stop by any time with little to no warning?

_____

_____

Who are your most helpful, friendliest neighbors?

_____

_____

Who stays most often in your guest room?

_____

_____

Who are some of the best houseguests you've hosted?

_____

_____

_____

Who can always be counted on to show up for support, comfort, and care during challenging times?

_____

_____

_____

Who would you trust to watch your house?

_____

_____

_____

Which of your kids' friends always bring happiness to your house? The ones you'd go above and beyond to help? Are you friends with their parents, and what is your time spent together like?

_____

_____

_____

_____

_____

_____

Who are your household dream-team members, and what's special about them?

_____

_____

_____

_____

Babysitters

_____

_____

Nannies

_____

_____

Au pairs

_____

_____

Dog-walkers

_____

_____

Petsitters

_____

_____

Housecleaning specialists

_____

_____

Handymen

_____

_____

Mail carriers

_____

_____

Lawn service professionals

_____

_____

Others

_____

_____

If you're lucky enough to have parents and grandparents who offer to help with projects around your house, what have they worked on with you?

_____

_____

_____

Who are the first people you add to a party invitation list?

_____

If you belong to a book club, or other groups that meet in your home for a shared activity or event, what are those groups like?

_____

_____

Who else adds to the richness of this house just by being here?

_____

What we do in this house on rainy weekend days:

_____

_____

What we do in this house on rainy nights:

_____

_____

What we do in this house on snowy weekend days:

_____

_____

What we do in this house on snowy nights:

_____

_____

What we do in this house on perfect fall days:

_____

_____

What we do in this house on perfect warm days:

_____

_____

What are the best sounds of this house? (Examples include visitors laughing, music playing, singing, whistling, or your beloved dog barking. Even the familiar little creak of the front door opening can sound like music when you love a place this much.)

_____

_____

_____

_____

What are the best things we've seen in this house? (Examples include rainbows; shooting stars; meteors; the Milky Way; the northern lights; deep snowfalls and drifts that look like waves on a lake; or animals you don't normally see around here like bears, coyotes, mountain lions, and so many beautiful birds on their migration routes. How did nature deliver her magic to you?)

_____

_____

_____

_____

Is there anything else that encapsulates what you are like in this house, how you spend your time, how you plan your days, and how you share them with your favorite people? Journal those priceless memories, silly inside jokes, the favorite cozy seats in the house, and anything else you can think of.

Someday, you and your loved ones might be reading about this house while you're not in it, after you've moved on. Come here to travel back in time, feel yourself reading on the couch with your babies or jumping up and spilling snack mix everywhere because of an unexpected interception in the big game. . . . You get to go back because *you wrote it all down.*

When a loved one passes away and you miss them terribly, you can come back to these moments of cheering loudly, high fives, digging into that impossibly good chili that Dad made, clapping along to stadium music even though you're not in the stadium . . . by flipping through this book. You feel like you're right back with that loved one again as you take in those memories.

Notes:

_____

_____

_____

_____

_____

_____

_____

_____

_____

_____

Chapter 8

Kids' Moments

Oh, what a sweet chapter this is! You may have posted just about everything of your kids' lives on your social media accounts, but those are . . . social media accounts. Typed. Probably unconsciously shaped by the knowledge that these posts are for other people to see and comment on. The memories in this book aren't for public consumption, nor are they tailored to the usual stylings of social media posts. This chapter is all about the happiness and fun of your children's lives *here in this house.*

The Babies

Bringing home a baby is a momentous occasion. Those little eyes may not be able to see too clearly just yet, but you know that baby is checking out this house of yours. He or she has come quite a distance and can now know that *this is my house. I am home.*

Attach photos of baby's nursery here.

Gather some of each of your babies' firsts in this house. (Add more pages if needed.)

	BABY 1	BABY 2	BABY 3
First Smile			
First finger gripped (Whose was it?)			
First time standing up (Where did this happen?)			
First steps (Where did this happen?)			
First word			
First favorite thing			
Other first			

Baby, oh baby, getting used to life in this house!

As Kids Grow

Soon you have a little speedster zipping around the house, climbing on couches, chasing pets, and even dancing. Speaking of dancing, what were some of your kids' favorite songs at different ages?

CHILD (AND AGE)	FAVORITE SONG

CHILD (AND AGE)	FAVORITE SONG

What about favorite books? List the first books they read themselves, their favorite series, and their favorite books you read together here in this house.

CHILD (AND AGE)	FAVORITE BOOK OR SERIES

Now let's see the kids' rooms as they grow.

Attach photos here.

Where are your children's favorite places to be in the house? Perhaps it's the top bunk or a beanbag chair where he reads his books. Maybe it's a backyard playhouse or her spot on the couch where she can snuggle with you.

What are your children's favorite everyday foods, snacks, and special foods?

What are the first things your kids helped you cook, bake, or prepare? (Cookies? Pancakes?)

What were the first things your children ever cooked or prepared solo?

What would your kids absolutely not eat, to the point that it's a very big deal?

What are your kids' favorite restaurants?

_____

_____

What are your kids' favorite pizza toppings?

_____

_____

KIDS' BIRTHDAYS AND PARTIES

You may recall some of your own birthday parties from when you were a little kid. Of course, they stick in your mind when you get that kind of magic on your birthday. Maybe you had a soccer-themed party, a princess party, a zoo-themed celebration, or perhaps a family bowling night at the local lanes. If you had a deployed parent, you might have done the bowling night as a little something fun but saved the theme party for when your mom or dad came home. That's a birthday you'll remember.

Here is where you can journal those standout birthday parties you threw for your little ones. The parties you put your all into planning, crafting, cooking, or calling for special treats.

Your kids can fill in details here, as an excellent record of what _they_ loved most, and their answers might surprise you. Maybe you thought that the mermaid-themed party you planned had stellar décor, but it was really the sushi that the kids went wild over, as well as the dollar-store jeweled hairclips you provided for the birthday child and as party favors.

> This book is going to keep surprising you when you look back on it later, both with what you do and don't remember and especially what your loved ones choose to write here.

Kid: _____

Birthday #: _____

Location: _____

Theme: _____

Décor: _____

Menu: _____

_____

_____

Cake: _____

Games: _____

_____

Favors: _____

Who attended: _____

_____

_____

_____

Best moments: _____

_____

Or add a photo here.

Kid: _____

Birthday #: _____

Location: _____

Theme: _____

Décor: _____

Menu: _____

_____

_____

Cake: _____

Games: _____

_____

Favors: _____

Who attended: _____

_____

_____

_____

Best moments: _____

_____

Or add a photo here.

Kid: _____

Birthday #: _____

Location: _____

Theme: _____

Décor: _____

Menu: _____

_____

_____

Cake: _____

Games: _____

_____

Favors: _____

Who attended: _____

_____

_____

_____

Best moments: _____

_____

Or add a photo here.

Kid: _____

Birthday #: _____

Location: _____

Theme: _____

Décor: _____

Menu: _____

_____

_____

Cake: _____

Games: _____

_____

Favors: _____

Who attended: _____

_____

_____

_____

Best moments: _____

_____

Or add a photo here.

Kid: _____

Birthday #: _____

Location: _____

Theme: _____

Décor: _____

Menu: _____

_____

_____

Cake: _____

Games: _____

_____

Favors: _____

Who attended: _____

_____

_____

_____

Best moments: _____

_____

 *Or add a photo here.*

What were some of the biggest "wow factor" birthday details you can remember from the parties you planned for your children? It doesn't matter which kid's birthday it was or how old they were. Some years feel like milestone birthdays, and you just want to go big. Perhaps by having a local zoo bring a menagerie of animals to your property, like ponies with ribbons braided into their manes walking slow circles around your lawn. Maybe the "reptile guy" held court over the wide-eyed kids as he pulled baby alligators and snakes out of bins. Or maybe you hired a half dozen character actors in superhero outfits, fighting the bad guys in a "play" that included the kids. *You really know how to plan a party. Everyone says so.*

Go overboard here, too, to capture those amazing details and party personalizations. Don't forget the surprises and party rescues, like running out to a supermarket to replace a cake that hit the deck on a too-warm day.

What made kids' birthdays unforgettable?

How far in advance did you start planning kids' birthdays?

What were some birthday party–planning memories that your kids would love to hear about now?

What were some birthday party themes you're most proud of?

_____

_____

_____

Best homemade birthday party items? Balloon sculptures? Costumes? Stages?

_____

_____

_____

Additional kids' birthday party standout details:

_____

_____

_____

What do _other_ people remember and rave about your kids' birthday parties at your house?

_____

_____

_____

_____

And then there are slumber parties. The rite of passage that your kid either wants desperately or would pay you, if they could, not to make them attend. How did the old bra-in-the-freezer stunt endure for decades? Why did everyone want to be light as a feather, stiff as a board? Those antics may be long gone in favor of making TikToks and gaming, everyone chin down looking at their phones. Write here about the slumber parties that took place in your home, what food you served, what was a hit at the party, and what was the biggest drama among several dramas that night? Don't forget to record whether or not you crept outside to discover the teenage boys sneaking around in the shadows, hoping to meet up with the girls whose parents thought they were asleep on your floor. Slumber parties are an activity for parents as well.

Standout slumber party memories here in this house?

_____

_____

_____

Was anything that occurred so funny, but you had to hide your smiles from the kids?

_____

_____

_____

What are some things you "accidentally" overheard from the slumber party kids?

_____

_____

_____

Did you have an all-family slumber party or campout in the backyard?

_____

_____

_____

WHEN THERE WAS A PARTY AND YOU WEREN'T HOME

You: Did you have a party while we were away?

Yes. They did.

If you can find any evidence, or if you get calls from parents about their hungover math-letes and cheerleaders, this is where that little time capsule snapshot goes.

Attach photos here. Lots of them.
It's best if you arrive home early, during the party. Kids.

Ask your kids to list or describe their own favorite memories in this house.

_____

_____

_____

_____

_____

_____

_____

_____

What are your favorite memories with your kids in this house?

_____

_____

_____

_____

_____

_____

_____

_____

Chapter 9

Pets of the House

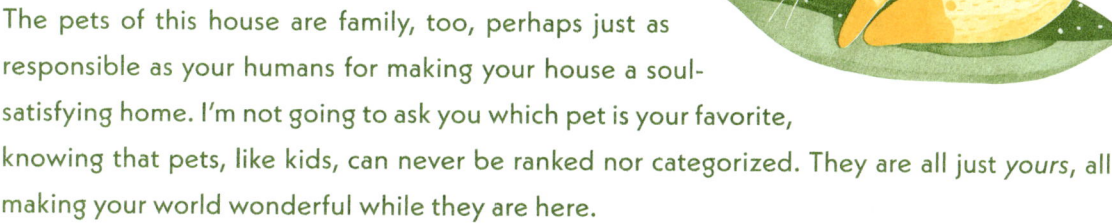

The pets of this house are family, too, perhaps just as responsible as your humans for making your house a soul-satisfying home. I'm not going to ask you which pet is your favorite, knowing that pets, like kids, can never be ranked nor categorized. They are all just *yours*, all making your world wonderful while they are here.

There's no way to fully describe the feeling of a puppy's first licks on your face.

Or the warmth of a dog on your lap, gently snoring as he sleeps. In the happiest place he knows.

A kitten's first climb up the curtains. You want to be mad, but it's just so cute!

Pets look at you like you hung the moon and scattered the stars, and they simply create a different level of connection in your world. It's pure love.

Give your pets' memories their due here, and show anyone who might look upon your life stories how much your pets were adored.

Did you bring a pet or pets into this home when you originally moved in? Journal everything about your original darling(s).

What was the first new pet in this home?

_____

Share some details on how your family found and named this pet.

_____

_____

What are your pets' names, and what/who are they named after?

_____

_____

Describe what your pets are like in this house. Does he sleep in a sunbeam on the wood floor? Does she wait by the window for the kids' school bus to pull up?

_____

_____

What is your pet's favorite treat?

_____

_____

Who is your pet's favorite person? Some pets don't go by the rules of human parents in not favoring one kid over the other. Your pet might have a very clear preference for one member of your family. This favoritism becomes family lore.

_____

_____

_____

Pet Halloween costumes—you either love them or hate them, and your pet either obliges or fights you to *get that thing off him*. What are some of your favorite pet costumes over the years?

_____

_____

Which pet did you have for the longest time?

_____

What are/were your most unusual pets?

_____

Which pet does the best tricks?

_____

_____

Who are your rescue pets?

_____

_____

What are your "things we do for our pets" stories, like home cooking organic food to meet your pet's nutritional needs? Driving everywhere to look for the pet shampoo your dog prefers? Adopting another pet so that your pet has a friend?

_____

_____

_____

Which pet is your most mischievous?

_____

_____

Which pet has the most attitude?

_____

_____

Share your best pet stories here—with photos.

Chapter 10

Weather Wonders

Superstorms, hurricanes, and all manner of destructive storms aside (and perhaps you don't even want to remember those!), there's a degree of loveliness that comes to life in your house thanks to the weather. When it rained, perhaps you slipped on your ponchos and went for a walk. When it snowed, perhaps you stepped outside during the night to listen to the faint sounds of light sleet bouncing on the snow, when everything else in the moonlight was still, silent, and peaceful.

Perhaps you shared those moments with your family members.

With so much of life being so noisy and frenetic, your house pulsing with music and loud talking, life going on boisterously in every room—and you wouldn't have it any other way—the silence of a crisp, fresh snowfall and the patter of raindrops on the skylights give you a chance to pause and catch your breath, even if just for a moment or two. When you think about it, the weather has been a backdrop to so many of your life's moments here in this house.

In this little chapter, note your weather memories. Maybe it's a breathtaking amount of snow on your property, five-foot-long icicles, a rainbow that arched through the sky during the simplest of drizzles, the bend of strong trees during high winds, and of course, the colors of autumn leaves and spring blooms.

What are your best weather-related memories during your time in this house?

Attach photos here.

What is your norm during thunderstorms? Cuddling up on the couch and reading? Or turning up the music to mask some of that howling wind?

_____

_____

_____

_____

_____

How does your group play in the rain?

_____

_____

_____

How do you play in the snow? Does your lawn provide any sledding excitement?

_____

_____

_____

Does your property offer any ice skating possibilities?

_____

_____

_____

_____

_____

Note your family members' best seasonal, weather-related memories, such as shoveling an elderly neighbor's walkway and driveway just before sunrise so that it would be a fresh surprise for them. Or dancing in the rain. Or helping clean away fallen tree branches after a storm, as neighbors arrived with their chainsaws and axes to help your family clear away the mess.

If you're the type to look through a weather challenge to see the blessings on the other side, thanks to helpful neighbors and kind friends, record here what you went through, who was there for you, and what the experience meant to you.

_____

_____

_____

_____

_____

_____

_____

_____

_____

_____

_____

_____

_____

_____

Chapter 11

Researching the History of This House

A house tells its own story, no matter how old it is. A house may have many stories to tell, since its origins during the Revolutionary War, while other homes tell the story of a new construction. Everywhere around you, your house exhales its history, and even the land your house sits on has much to reveal.

For instance, when my husband and I moved into our house, we found in our attic the not-very-preserved, yellowed wedding dress of the eighty-something-year-old woman from whom we bought the house. Next to that was an impressive collection of John F. Kennedy assassination-themed *Life* magazines and newspapers. Neat finds.

While planting maple trees in our front yard, my husband dug up a large number of very old red bricks, some of them burnt to ash on the sides as if they had been part of a fireplace at one time. There was no maker's mark, no uniform ridging, and the mortar between the bricks was grainy, encrusted with what looked like burnt birdseed. What did our front lawn used to be? A field hospital long ago? A blacksmith's forge? These bricks held a story, and thus began our search for details on our home's history.

Your House's Past and Who Slept in Your Home Office

If it's not something buried in the yard that gets you researching your home's history, it might be the fact that you live in a historic neighborhood where buildings may have been saloons, or that mansion on the hill may have been part of a historically infamous Millionaire's Row of grand estates with jaw-dropping design details and grounds to envy, with juicy stories of long-ago passions and parties and perhaps a little bit of crime. For instance, if you're a fan of the musical *Hamilton*, you may be thrilled to find out that Alexander Hamilton himself stayed in many now-historic homes, and if you can identify the estates near you, you may discover that Hamilton may have at least glanced in your home's direction, if not spent the night in the room that is now your home office. Those who research a house's history find out things like that.

You're more likely to find the letters, photos, and miscellaneous items of everyday people of a past era. Their artifacts and beautifully handwritten notes give you a glimpse into their realities, how people addressed one another, and what mattered to those who thought *then* to write things down. The stories of your home include *their* stories.

Regular people just living their lives in fascinating times leave some fabulous clues of what a different era was like. For instance, if you find a receipt or a note stowed in your basement along with some cloudy but gorgeous glass bottles, Prohibition may be giving you a wink. Local places, you may find, have astonishing histories as speakeasies where mobsters were once regulars, ladies drank Bee's Knees cocktails, and secret passwords were spoken at the door.

Matching your home to a different era's local history and culture can be illuminating.

Even if you don't have former speakeasies and Gatsby-style rows of mansions where the wealthy families from the big city used to "summer" nearby, your area is just as rich in sentiment. Perhaps the history you find in your home is simply a sweet love story of a couple married seventy years who slow-danced by the fireplace, held hands wherever they went, planted a lush English garden outside, and died peacefully a day apart. "He would have followed her anywhere" reads the handwritten note in a sympathy card you find among their ephemera in the attic. How beautiful to know that such love lived here!

YOUR HOUSE'S TILES AND BONES

Researching the history of your home becomes a fascinating, and perhaps *profitable*, literal "house hunt" when you're looking closely at the tile design in the backsplash of your stovetop, or the pattern of tile in your shower, on the bathroom walls, and on the outdoor patio. These tiny elements of tiled design have been in your eyeline and underfoot for years, and you may never have known that they are among the most searched-for, hard-to-get, vintage tiles. If you've found a box of unused tiles in the basement, you may have discovered a few thousand dollars' worth of sellable treasures that another remodeling homeowner would celebrate finding.

You're going a few steps beyond "What a fascinating story!" to "What is this neat vintage tile worth if we want to sell it?" Get up close to all the elements that make up your home—those amazing windows or the barn door in the shed that's worth a *lot* to home remodelers—and you'll find layers of potential in more ways than you think. Yes, being able to sell your original cabinets, hardware, windows, and even your antique doorknobs for impressive amounts on the thrifting circuit lets you build your cash pile for the remodels you're aiming for. Or they just help stockpile a bundle of cash for your savings.

> Money aside, here's your house telling a story, showing you clues as to how it used to be and how it might be again.

Another benefit of looking up the history of your home is being educated about home details, products, styles, and safety issues when you're talking with contractors and artisans. A house's bones and design features may need an overlay of better features and stylish décor, and your house has a lot to say about what can be done. It's a fascinating partnership. You're going to learn the most wonderful things about your house!

DIVING DEEP INTO YOUR HOUSE'S HISTORY

You can do quite a bit of research on your house's history yourself, but additional help might be beneficial, too. The remainder of this chapter shows you where to look as you research the history of your home.

Google

Of course, your search starts here. When you want to get right to it, information is just a quick Google search away. It's a good starting point. Start off by googling your home address, and if it's not a new build, you'll find real estate sites with your home's previous listings. Here is where you'll find the types and sizes of your rooms most recently . . . and *what they used to be*. Older listings reveal not just what you paid for your house, but what the prior owners paid for their time here, and when home modifications started showing up in listings. There's hardwood floor beneath your carpet and tile. That third floor? It was added in the 1970s. These property listings, and links to find the older ones, tell so many stories about what your house was like throughout the decades.

You'll likely find additional good stuff further down in the search results. That's where you may see mentions of your home specifically if you've had, say, garage sales or if there was ever an estate sale in your house's history. If a notable resident lived in your home, you may find a fascinating little gem of a mention in a basic Google search.

Next, plug your address into Google Images to see photos of your property through the years. A grainy, black-and-white photo may show that there was once no house next to your place, that a sunny, wildflower-filled lot extended to the trees and a stream. The neighborhood kids used to play there. In the photos of your house, you might see that you used to have a wraparound porch long ago. Or that your driveway was on the other side of the house but the township moved it so it would be up to code and give you the street address you have now. If your driveway remained on the other side of the corner lot you're on, you'd have a different address! Old photos might show the previous residents and their kids, perhaps playing in that field.

These easy, first searches often turn up some amazing clues, energizing your search for fascinating FYIs and hopefully some interesting photos.

Public Records

Deeds, liens, and lawsuits each tell a story, perhaps of struggle and overcoming. Or maybe they just offer a wellspring of names, occupations, family members, kids, and losses of loved ones. Your house's rich history embraces the stories of the people who've come before you, whose names you may see handwritten on marriage certificates, on titles, and as signatures on forms and petitions, all of which are sources of information. That baby in the porch photo? She may live in your town now, perhaps in the retirement home two miles away, ready to celebrate her ninetieth birthday. Her granddaughter lives *in your neighborhood*, you discover, because her grandfather *designed* this neighborhood long ago. The streets are named after all of his daughters and sons. The street where your house sits is named after her.

Make it a goal to find the origin of your street name. When developers have the opportunity to name streets, they often choose the names of their loved ones; historical figures; objects of nature such as lakes, ponds, and mountains; and—interestingly—references to what *used* to be in this space. For instance, Church Lane is a nod to an actual church that served as the center of the community long ago. Someone, at some point in time, likely wrote that down.

Public records are kept at a number of different agencies and departments, so inquire at the following:

- Tax assessor's office
- Town hall
- County recorder
- Department of Buildings
- Department of Public Safety
- Census data office. Census data is also found at the U.S. Census Bureau's website, census.gov; your public library; and a number of websites you can find via Google. Stick with the official sites, for your safety, and don't enter your personal and financial information into sites you don't know are secure.
- National Register of Historic Places. The U.S. National Park Service website features the National Register of Historic Places at nps.gov/subjects/nationalregister/index.htm. Here you can look up many states' historic places registries. Or you can check your state's official website for a link to your state's register of historic places and homes. Again, wherever you look and whatever sites you log onto, protect your personal information.
- Your local library. A reference librarian can direct you to safe sites for searching homes' histories and even help you look up information on the people who used to live there.

Your Public and County Libraries

Speaking of libraries, they have *the goods*. Not only can you access files of town newspapers from the 1800s to the present, but you can find old maps as well, and old maps contain far more information than you might expect. People *frame* these old maps as art, they're so beautiful and detailed. But when you find old maps of your local area, you're going to see lines showing the *land parcels* from long-ago families who owned big segments of your area. The family name might already be familiar to you through local lore, or the names might be breadcrumbs to the next fascinating discovery.

When I looked up my house's footprint on an old map, I saw just a woman's name. *There has to be a story here*, I thought, because in 1899, it was uncommon to find a single female landowner. What I found through the library was that Miss Amelia was a wealthy woman who never married, and the home she built on this land—our land—was the site of summery parties and society socializing. It's exactly the kind of history I was hoping to find. And I likely would not have found it without my local library. So, Miss Amelia, feel free to check out what we're doing here on the land you loved. We're pleased to meet you now.

Another surprising thing I discovered about my local library was that I could call the library, tell them that I'm researching the history of my house, and they would *offer me a library worker as a research assistant. For free.* I told our researcher what I had so far, and she set off collecting, returning to us six or seven big boxes of *collections*. Old photos from our neighborhood and local areas, old maps, journals from families in the area with *entries about being in our house (!)*. We saw a lot of budget books listing handwritten items bought at the local general store, prices in pennies, and a ledger of who paid what when. In times of influenza and other hardships like tough winters, the shopping list was fascinating. Home remedies like cabbage for sore joints. Lots of twine and cheesecloth for winter cheese-making. Fabric for making a burial dress. Faded calling cards with the names of "members of society" on them. Dried flowers and fabric bows.

The library's boxes of collections also contain the papers of notable families in the area, and (thrilling!) the materials lists for the building the engineers were working on long ago that *still stands today.* Architecture details abound in library collections. Along with them, handwritten poetry and short stories live in a simple manila folder, the founders' artistic inspirations sharing space with their architectural ideas.

Someone took the time to write it all down and then donate it to the library . . . which is where you'll find it and be able to sift through the pieces that connect to your house and its place in the region.

What do you need to tell your librarian?

That you're researching the history of your house.

The address, town location in block and lot numbers, and any lot drawings showing your house's positioning on the land. Your lot may be one of ten lots broken off from an estate, after all, so you want to pinpoint your parcel.

What you've researched so far, even if it's just a run-through of a few top real estate sites.

Any names you've been able to discover in your house's and area's history.

That you've found artifacts, like cloudy glass bottles found in your basement; bricks from your backyard that may perfectly match a long, winding brick fence along the outer edges of the estate's property; or lengths of wood that might have been a dock. Show them photos of these finds.

What you are hoping to discover, including any topics of personal interest, such as finding out if a hospital, school, or encampment site once existed here. Perhaps you've seen some peculiar shadows or heard something strange in the winds at night, and you just *have* to get some questions answered. Or perhaps you've heard that Gold Rush prospectors once populated your area, and you'd like to find some documentation of what they might have experienced or found here.

How much you appreciate your library staff's help with your research. Baked goods and gift cards are always a nice idea for thank-you gifts.

Historical Society

The library can point you toward your state's historical society or the American Historical Association if you find that your house has some historic notoriety, and the process of listing and protecting your property as a national landmark can begin. Or you might find that many years ago, your home was named as a property worthy of historic landmark status. When named as a property on the historic registry, your home may qualify as a place worthy of historic preservation. So your columned porch might get some attention and repair love from the historical society, and add even more to the stories of your house.

Ask the Neighbors

Mention your house research to any neighbors you know because someone in the neighborhood may know the people who used to live in your house. Maybe they moved out of state decades ago, but the mother of someone in your book club still keeps in touch with them. Don't be shy. Write a letter explaining that you're doing some research into the stories of your home and would be interested in any information they might be able to share, such as the love stories of people who used to live there and any fascinating achievements and unexpected FYIs.

> **Tip:** When you tell others that you're looking for the *stories* of the people and the house, the person you're writing to out of the blue may relax a bit, sensing that you're just a sweet family curious about your house's history, not some kind of insurance adjuster looking to find out more about the faulty screws on the stairs they put in years ago. Put them at ease by crafting a brief letter of request for any stories. Offer to stop by with coffee and cookies for a short visit. Make this one of those lovely little personal interactions that add to the stories of the house.

Here's an example of a letter requesting information on the house:

Hello, Martha and David! We are Anne and Michael from 155 B Street, just up the road from you. We're researching the history of our house right now, and we hear that you might have some interesting stories about when this neighborhood was built, who lived in our house and what were they like, and what was nearby. If you'd be interested in chatting, please do let us know! Our phone number is 973-555-1212. Thank you!

Granted, people may be wary of strangers asking them for anything these days, but you may find a serendipitous connection that reveals so many wonderful little details about your house's history. You may find out who to thank (even silently) for planting your yard's most stately trees.

Neighbors know the stories. You may even find multiple people happy to introduce you to families connected to your home's origins. Your research takes off from there.

Chapter 12

Leaving This House

When your time in this house is over and you're ready to move on to your next home, your next adventure, it can be surprisingly hard to say goodbye to this house, which has kept you safe and comforted for all these years. That sigh of relief when you finally get home after a long trip or an exhausting event signals your reconnection to the safe zone where your soul feels unclenched. *I'm home. Our home.* It's a deep love.

Add to that the many layers of deep love your family members feel for this house. They, too, cherish all the big family moments in your home. They love their own space in it. They share many of your memories and have so many more of their own that you might not know about or remember. If they haven't initiated this move, they're likely pretty devastated, especially if they weren't prepared for how hard it would be to say goodbye to this house, their old, dear friend.

This could be very hard on you, too.

Or you might be popping bottles of champagne because you're now on your way to a new dream, a new house, a new life. There's a mountain of emotions in that as well.

Record your thoughts on leaving this house, what you take with you, and what you leave behind.

Moving is a rite of passage. A passage is a way, route, channel, opening, path, course. It's also a chapter, an episode. A way through. You're stepping off the secure and trusted ground of your home and into a moving reality peppered with unknowns. *It's a lot.* So take some time to reflect on the following questions as you process this transition.

What inspired you to sell this house?

_____

_____

_____

What have you loved most about living in this house?

_____

_____

_____

What did this house teach you?

_____

_____

_____

You're a different person now than you were when you first moved here. How does it feel to be a different person saying goodbye to this space? What would the "old you" say about leaving this house?

_____

_____

_____

_____

_____

_____

Including people and pets, how many loved ones have lived here at one time or another? How many friends have moved through this space?

_____

_____

_____

_____

Which physical items are you taking from this home? A doorknob? A leftover tile from when you remodeled the bathroom?

_____

_____

_____

Which items are you taking with you in the form of photos and video, such as the height markers on the door that measure how much the kids have grown, or a love message written to you on the inside of your closet?

_____

_____

_____

What were your house's "weird things," such as that one basement step that always seemed just a little bit too angled or strange noises that you could never place?

_____

_____

_____

What will you miss most about this house?

_____

_____

_____

What is your plan for saying goodbye? A champagne toast? Everyone says a few words? Record your ideas here.

_____

_____

_____

What message do you have for the house? Say thank you for the years of love and protection this house has given you by writing a farewell letter to your home.

_____

_____

_____

_____

_____

_____

_____

_____

_____

A Note for Future Generations

Write a letter to future generations of your family about your life in this home. Surely there are some details that go beyond the questions I've asked here. Maybe it's the influence that family elders had in this home, items they made by hand and gifted to you, or their advice in letters and conversations. Or maybe it's traditions and habits that your family would know deep in their souls. No one could ask the right questions to bring those gems out of you. Only you would know. So open these pages whenever you're daydreaming about relatives or ancestors, to create a bridge between them and *future* generations.

Allow future generations to see and feel your life in this house.

Reveal where the secret items are hidden beneath floorboards, behind drywall, in cornices, or in crown molding. Tell them where the treasures are planted in the yard or where overgrown foliage might obscure a memorial or garden stone with particular interest. Give them the insider secrets VIP tour of your house's history.

This book and this letter become a treasure map that allows your future loved ones to gaze into any room and open their minds to a gauzy dream sequence they can visualize for themselves of your happy family prepping dinner together as the family dog rests at your feet. Let them hear your favorite dinner prep playlist. Let them imagine some of the magic that took place in your house.

This detail. These images. They're all part of the stories of this house, and the memories will live on with future generations because you wrote it all down.

A Note for Future Generations

A Note to Leave for the Next Owners

This is just a little something to leave for the next owners of your home. It can be a brief, two-line note saying, "Welcome home! We had a very happy life here, this house has been so wonderful to us, and now we wish you every happiness and dream come true here! Xoxo"

This kind of note soars in its simplicity.

These are people you likely don't know, so they don't need a ten-page letter from you. Short and sweet is always best as a welcome note for the new owners.

A Note from the Author

I was very lucky to get to know my parents' house's new owners and their dog.

When they remodeled the house, they invited my husband and me to walk through their newly renovated kitchen, which now spanned what used to be three separate rooms; the family room, which had just enjoyed some fresh paint and a fireplace refresh; and all the bedrooms, which looked bright and stylish.

I was happy for the house.

It had such bright energy in it, a kitchen meant for entertaining large groups, the most wonderful color palette, and a scented warmth. It was everything I could ever have wanted for that house. My parents, from their viewpoint up above, would be happy for their house as well.

Additional Notes Pages

I couldn't possibly capture everything about your house in this journal's prompts. It's your home and reflects you and your family's hearts, personalities, traditions, and ways you all have evolved over time. So I'm including extra pages for notes, scribbled memories, big moments that everyone in your house wants to share, and additional photos.

You'll write here when inspiration strikes, coming back to it when you are flipping through to revisit your life in this house. You'll write here when posting stories about your family on Facebook feels too much like bragging, or too incomplete, or like those social media posts don't really get to the heart of what feels great about family time.

This is where your memories will live. You'll add to them today, tomorrow, maybe years from now . . . and your loved ones may smile, finding this book in your attic or in a box in the back of the closet someday, getting exactly what they need: answers to so many little questions they never thought to ask you. Like, which great-aunt was it who made the almond torte for Christmas dinner. (*It was Aunt Tee. Short for Theresa. And the almond torte recipe is in this book.*)

Here, you'll make up your own topics and questions about your life in this house and record the responses in your own handwriting. Because to your loved ones, your *handwriting* is everything.

Additional Notes and Photos of Life in This House

Additional Notes and Photos of Life in This House

Additional Notes and Photos of Life in This House

Additional Notes and Photos of Life in This House

Additional Notes and Photos of Life in This House

Additional Notes and Photos of Life in This House

01 14

Additional Notes and Photos of Life in This House

Additional Notes and Photos of Life in This House